MIDGES
IN
SCOTLAND

GEORGE HENDRY

Cartoons by *BAX*

BIRLINN

This fifth edition published in 2011 by
Birlinn Limited
West Newington House
10 Newington Road
Edinburgh
EH9 1QS
www.birlinn.co.uk

First published April 1989 by Aberdeen University Press
Second edition published 1996, third edition 2000 and fourth edition
2003 by Mercat Press

ISBN-13: 978 1 84158 938 1
eBook ISBN: 978 0 85790 102 6

British Library Cataloguing-in-Publication Data
A catalogue record for this book is available from the British Library

Typeset in Ehrhardt at Birlinn

Printed and bound in Great Britain by Bell & Bain Ltd., Glasgow

CONTENTS

ACKNOWLEDGEMENTS

Midges in Scotland, now in its fifth edition, continues to thrive alongside its insect subject-matter, despite trumpeted claims for devices which kill midges by the kilo or repellents which offer midge-free summers. Despite what they say on the bottle, midges still rule, particularly in the Scottish Highlands.

The origins of the book go back to a difficult period in my university research as a biochemist. As leader of a small research team, our laboratory studies were beset with technical problems, research grants were uncertain, the builders were installing central heating and I personally needed a break. I had long had an interest in the way that blood, haemoglobin to be precise, was broken down during digestion—whether by mosquitoes, ticks or in human diet. I also had an old house in the Highlands to which I would retreat. The house, by coincidence, was just down the road from the site of the Government's post-war field trials with the aim of countering the midges. The combination of the Highland house, haemoglobin and the need for a break in what turned out to be a particularly midgy summer led naturally enough to the book.

Twenty years later, research into midges in Scotland and elsewhere suffers, as always, from lack of funding. However, in the years elapsed since the last edition, our understanding of midges has improved a little and the effect that changing climates may have on midge activity continues to alter our perspective. Although the search for new ways to repel midges occasionally exercises the mind of the pharmaceutical industry, in recent years it has been more rewarding to see many visitors to the Highlands learning to acquire the art of living with midges. This new edition brings the story up to date.

Five editions and several updates of this book have only been possible with the advice and support from colleagues working in the field, and laboratory, on midges in various parts of the world. In particular I would like to acknowledge the generous help I have received from Alison Blackwell, John Boorman, Art Borkent, Douglas Kettle, Veronica Mands, Philip Mellor, Bill and Jenny Mordue and Angus Stewart. As before, I have not identified the work of the individual contributions within the text. They will no doubt recognise their part within these pages. I also thank the many readers who have taken the trouble to tell me of their own experiences. Standing on the sideline watching a village shinty match on a warm summer's evening in the Highlands is a great occasion to be regaled by tales of midges. Some of these accounts are recorded here.

My thanks to Tom Johnstone of Birlinn for his encouragement and patience, and to Ishy Hendry for the life–cycle drawing.

Balnacra, Ross-shire

PREAMBLE

For years there has been a wee conspiracy that the midges should never be discussed in front of the tourists. By mentioning not a word about midges in the holiday-guides to Scotland, let alone giving simple advice on living with midges, in some way it is hoped that the midge problem will go away. Unfortunately, the midges will not go away and, year after year, the visitors are driven to distraction and even to dislike the Scottish Highlands. Fortunately, many people do learn to live with the midges and to enjoy Scotland in all its seasons.

This account sets out to describe in fairly brief everyday terms how, when and why midges bite, to say something about their biology and to consider ways of avoiding the worst assaults of a midge pack hard on your scent. Over the years many attempts have been made to control midges, both in Scotland and overseas, occasionally with considerable success, more often with unexpected costs. Generally, the midge has the last word in these conflicts with Man. At the very least then, this book will give the visitor and Highlander alike the satisfaction of knowing their common enemy. By understanding the ways of the midge, a lot more people should be able to enjoy the full splendour of the Highland summer without quite so many bites!

INTRODUCTION

The proximity of the biting midge and the wearing of the kilt gave rise to the Highland fling! This is probably the only joke that can be made about an insect which has long been a curse of the Highland summers. Like its relative, the mosquito, it is the female midge which bites to secure a blood-meal for its developing eggs. Despite plagues of biting midges in the Canadian outback, in Siberia, on the sun-drenched beaches of Australia and the Caribbean, experienced travellers and zoologists alike agree that some of the fiercest midges in the world are to be found in the Highlands of Scotland. Wherever they abound in large numbers, midges cause discomfort, distress and some pain to warm-blooded animals, including humans. Social barriers they ignore. Attacks are made on the high and low with indifference. It was biting midges which half-devoured Queen Victoria at a Sutherland woodland picnic according to her diary of 1872 (perhaps in retribution for her visit to the memorial of the notorious James Loch in Dunrobin Wood, half an hour earlier).

Turning their attention to lesser mortals, midges were held responsible for serious delays in the building of the Krasnoyarsk dam in Siberia in 1960. Few insects have achieved front-page coverage in *Pravda* under the headline 'This evil can be conquered'! Back in Scotland, sixty years ago, both the Scottish Tourist Board and the Secretary of State for Scotland, Tom Johnston, sponsored scientific research into ways of combating midges. The outcome was to show that there were several profound and costly solutions to the midge problem and just a few rather simpler and cheaper answers. These simple answers rely on an understanding of the unusual lifestyle of the biting midge.

Man has dwelt in the Highlands for the last 8,000 years, maybe more, and has long learnt to live with all sorts of insect life and, for almost all of that time, without the aid of synthetic insecticides and repellents. Even today with our heightened expectations of carefree holidays, it is still possible to enjoy the Highlands without the support of these toxins and many people do just that. There can be few more extraordinary sights in the Highlands than to see travellers on the platform of Achnasheen Station waiting for the arrival of the 7.15 train on a warm summer's evening. Word has it that the local midges only get up for feeding 15 minutes before the train arrives. In that short interval they get to work to savage the tired, hot, defenceless traveller. But what of the friendly guard? He knows his midges all too well and does just what his forefathers have done for generations. Come 7.18 p.m., the train draws away for Kyle, and the Highlands each summer night are given over to the midges. These creatures form a dominant and successful part of Scottish wildlife and by controlling man's activities in the Highlands they are the guardians of some of the most beautiful and unspoilt areas of Northwest Europe. The Highlands would not be the same without the midges.

HISTORICAL PERSPECTIVE

The very word 'midge' is one originating deep in European prehistory, linked to the old Norse *my*, the *mygge* of the Swedes, the *mugge* of the Dutch, the *mycg* of the Saxons or, in Scots, mudge or midgeck. But despite its antiquity, the midge gets few references in the early literature of Scotland. Not one word is given by Tacitus in his account of his father-in-law Agricola's armed excursions into the Grampians around AD 80. One thing is certain, those bare sweating thighs of the Roman legions would have been sore bitten as they clacked their way through the wetlands of

Strathmore on their way north. Nor did the once proud English host at Bannockburn pause in their flight to describe what it was like to have midges nibbling away under chain-mail or surcoat on that warm June day in 1314. Midges indeed get little mention in the literature of the earlier centuries—particularly in Gaelic culture. Maybe this silence tells us something of our modern-day perceptions of insect life.

It is not until the eighteenth century that writers start to comment on midges in the Highlands. One of the first was Edward Burt, diarist and civil engineer to General Wade in Lochaber. He wrote in the 1730s from Fort Augustus, while resting from military road construction: 'I have been vexed with a little plague... swarms of little flies which the natives call Malhoulakins... being of a blackish colour when a number of them settle on the skin, they make it look dirty; there they bore with their little augers and change the face from black to red...' Burt himself was up on horseback while his road gangs presumably had to suffer *na chuileagan* without relief. Objectively he noted 'sometimes when I have been talking to any one, I have endured their stings to watch his face and see how long they would suffer him to be quiet; but in three to four seconds, he has slapped his hand upon his face and in great wrath cursed the little vermin'.

Bonnie Prince Charlie, hiding in the hills above Glen Moriston after his defeat at Culloden, may have escaped the Redcoats but never the midges—or, as one contemporary account had it, 'the evening being very calm and warm we greatly suffered by mitches, little creatures troublesome and numerous in the highlands... to preserve Him from such troublesome guests we wrapt him head and feet in his plaid, covered him with heather where he uttered several sighes and groans.' Weeks later in South Uist, the now less-than-bonny Teàrlach was in a terrible condition where 'the mitches devoured him and made him scratch those scars... made him appear as if he was covered with ulsers'. The entomological experiences of the 15,000 Government troops also out in the same heather looking for the prince are, however, unrecorded.

By the 1850s the Highlands had been opened up to gentlemen diarists, game fishers, artists and ultimately the royal family. C R Weld on a sketching tour was to write 'talk of solitude on the moors!—why, every square yard contains a population of millions of these little harpies, that pump blood out of you with amazing savageness and insatiability'.

Arguably, one of the most sustained midge assaults on sweating bare human flesh occurred in the first half of the nineteenth century with the construction, year after year, of the network of Parliamentary Roads across the west Highlands. Years later the military engineer Major General Colby recalled graphically how 'the heat being intense above Loch Maree and Gairloch and with our shirt necks thrown open and our sleeves tucked in we were exposed to the baneful attack of those venomous insects...our arms, necks and faces were covered with scarlet pimples and we lost several hours rest at night from the intense itching and pain. Even at the inns we had frequently to smoke in our bedrooms and over our meals to drive these insects away'. Doubtless the labour gangs, without access to inn bedrooms, fared even worse.

Midges figure in Scottish fiction. Indeed, at times good storytelling can capture more of the spirit of the Highlands than the raw factual account. Robert Louis Stevenson writing *Kidnapped* from sunny Bournemouth clearly had very real memories of the Highlands when he had Davie Balfour out on the heather much troubled by clouds of midges just before the shooting of the Red Fox, Colin Campbell of Glenure. The reader has to imagine the depth of determination that drove the assailant to hold steady aim with his flintlock with midges crawling over his arms, neck, ears and eyelids. The actual site of that murder, today deep in a Forestry Commission plantation near Ballachulish, holds the descendants of those midges in their ten thousands.

Likewise Neil Munro, writing of Para Handy safely from his Glasgow house, must have recalled his own childhood in Inveraray when he has the irrepressible Captain waxing fair on midges. He tells how on Colonsay an English 'chentleman' on his first night on the island went out in his kilt '...and came back in half an hour to the inns wi' his legs fair peetiful! There iss nothing that the mudges like to see among them than an English towerist with a kilt: the very top wass eaten off his stockins...' All this was put down to the Englishman's eccentricity in drinking ginger beer! In his travels up and down the west coast Para Handy and the crew of the *Vital Spark*, once outward from Bowling on the Clyde, experienced desperate midges in Bowmore on Islay, creatures repelled by paraffin in Rothesay on Bute, ones capable of biting through corrugated iron to get at flesh in Tighnabruaich, and midges from Dervaig on Mull with all the points of a Poltalloch terrier. But none could beat the solid wall of glutinous midges at Arrochar, at the head of Loch Fyne, where they numbered in billions, and where they were partial even to the strongest pipe tobacco smoke and considered paraffin a treat.

Scientific studies of the midge really began in the late nineteenth century in Britain, Belgium, Germany and Russia. By the 1930s much of the British midge fauna had been described in some detail in Edwards' blockbuster of a book *British Bloodsucking Flies* and later, in greater detail, in Campbell and Pelham-Clinton's classic account (see the Bibliography). (The second author was later honoured by the naming of a Scottish species first recognized in 1984 as *Culicoides clintoni*). In the years after the Second World War several more species were discovered lurking in the hills in Scotland including *C. scoticus, C. achrayi* (after Loch Achray in the Trossachs) and *C. duddingstoni* (after Duddingston Loch in Edinburgh). Today some thirty-five species of biting midge are known from Scotland (see the *Appendix*). However, as early as 1946 it was recognized that most of the attacks on humans were being carried out by just four or five species, of which one in particular was responsible for most of the trouble. This species enjoys the full scientific name of *Culicoides impunctatus* Goetghebuer, or more simply the Highland Midge.

The years immediately after the Second World War saw more research into midges in Scotland than at any time in the next half century, spurred by the vision of its Secretary of State for Scotland Tom Johnston and by the availability of the war-time anti-mosquito insecticides developed for use in south-east Asia.

By 1952 the University of Edinburgh had set up a Midge Control Unit specifically to study ways of combating the Highland Midge. Under the direction of Dr (later Professor) Douglas Kettle a great deal was learnt about the life of the midge in Scotland, and this work today forms the background for our understanding of the creature. Combined with the efforts of scientists in North and Central America, Australia, Russia and Britain, much is now known about midges, about their life-history, the way they reproduce, how they track their victims, in short what makes them such successful vicious little biters. The story that has emerged is a fascinating example of dedicated study frequently conducted under difficult and often painful conditions out on the hills and moors.

Ironically, from the 1960s with the post-war development of tourism in the Highlands, funding for sustained midge research in Scotland was allowed to lapse for over 30 years. In more recent times it has benefited significantly from a welcome (but, sadly, short-term) support to the universities of Aberdeen, Edinburgh and Dundee and the Institute of Animal Health which, together, have extended our knowledge of midge biology using modern techniques. Industry, including the repellent industry, has contributed relatively little towards long-term research—indeed privately-funded support has probably done more in this field in recent years than industry. Overseas, new technologies are being developed to combat disease-carrying sub-tropical pest species, particularly where they pose a possible threat to armed forces.

One simple message has emerged from this research, both at home and overseas. Almost all of the advances made in tackling the midge problem owe their successes to the groundwork needed to understand the life-history, the population dynamics, the behaviour, the physiology and the ecology of the insect. Without a sound understanding of how and why midges behave the way they do, then all the chemical sprayings, repellents and biological controls in the world become a waste of effort and money. The pity is that this simple message has not always been appreciated. Tourist boards, governments, local authorities, hoteliers and the tourists themselves want action and want it *now*. The trigger finger on the chemical spray-gun gets very twitchy. It is only when expensive eradication campaigns fail, often spectacularly, that the call for more research is finally heeded.

Modern man's almost instinctive urge to reach for his spray-gun has proved, time after time, to be a costly mistake. Midges are insects and like all other insects, as well as animals such as fish, birds or mammals, can be poisoned if enough toxins are thrown at them. Any chemical used against midges will, directly and indirectly, affect other harmless or even beneficial forms of life. It took twenty years of indiscriminate use of DDT both in North America and in Britain before this was recognized. Rachel Carson's book *Silent Spring*, which exposed the catastrophic effects on wildlife of the unregulated use of pesticides, had a profound effect on governments and scientists alike in the mid-1960s and today we have learnt to temper or suppress our urge to spray. The reward for striving for alternatives to chemical spraying, particularly in Central America and in Africa in the war against the mosquito and the tse-tse fly, has meant that today there are much more effective means of tackling insect pests and the diseases they carry, in ways which are less costly in money, more effective in improving human and animal health, and which achieve this without an indiscriminate destruction of the environment, including its wildlife. To appreciate how these modern approaches work it is necessary to understand something of the world of the midge. The accounts which follow can only be a summary. For those whose appetite is unsatisfied, the short bibliography at the end of the book will open a door to a fascinating world.

DISTRIBUTION

Biting midges are found world-wide and have exploited their peculiar talents over much of the land surface of the globe. Depending on geography, midges are known in different parts of the world as no-see-ums, punkies, moose-flies, sandflies or jejens. While many midge species exploit their diminutive size by preying on larger insects, others have evolved to feed undisturbed on a wide range of warm-blooded mammals or birds. Just a few have acquired a taste for human blood. Some 1,700 species of the most important genus *Culicoides* have been described so far, principally from sub-Arctic and temperate Europe, north and central America and Australia. The 1921 Everest climb met midges at 14,000 feet, while fugitive POW Heinrich Harrer was nabbed by midges on the shores of a Tibetan lake twenty years later. It is highly likely that many more undescribed species of midges exist in the tropics. Art Borkent working in the central American state of Costa Rica recently found over 300 species of biting midge new to science, in just one season of trapping.

In Scotland, what we lack in variety we make up for in numbers. Most of the thirty-five known Scottish species prey on cattle, sheep, horses and deer. A few confine their blood-sucking habits to domestic fowl and birds, and just four, or occasionally five, species attack humans. Most of the Scottish species have a characteristic, often local, distribution. Some restrict themselves to farm-yards and dung-heaps, others to sea or loch shores, a few to salt-marshes, mires or woodlands. Of the most persistent man-biters, just one species, *Culicoides impunctatus*, dominates in upland Britain, where it accounts for more than 90 per cent of the record-ed attacks. There has been some indication that the *C. impunctatus* population in Scotland may be a race distinct from the *C. impunc-tatus* midges found over the border in England and in continental Europe. If this can be proven it would go some way to explain why the midges of Scotland have such a vicious reputation.

The Scots who live in towns in the Lowlands have learnt to live with another species, *C. obsoletus* or the Garden Midge. There is nothing obsolete about the way this midge bites; it does so less painfully than its Highland cousin but it is infuriatingly persistent particularly behind a lawn-mower. This species can be found throughout Europe and Asia, and is widespread in Canada and the United States. A rather more painful biter, fairly com-mon on the Scottish salt-marshes and elsewhere, is likely to be *C. newsteadii* (known also as the beast of Arrochar), while on the croft in-bye another species, *C. nubeculosus*, will attack humans, particularly around stables, byres, fanks and among closely packed cattle and sheep. There are several other midge species which will have a go at humans from time to time but they are rarely much trouble. It remains true, however, that no natural habitat or loca-tion in Scotland can be considered to be entirely midge free. Bit-ing episodes in the hills above 1,500 feet may be reduced, but in sheltered corries midges can be active at considerable elevations. Nor is water a barrier. No less than three species of midge have been recorded from St Kilda, lying out in the Atlantic nearly 100 miles from the Scottish mainland. Only in densely developed cit-ies and towns are midges generally considered to be a trivial nui-sance, though even there the Garden Midge can get a hold on town parks and golf courses in wet summers. The banks of the

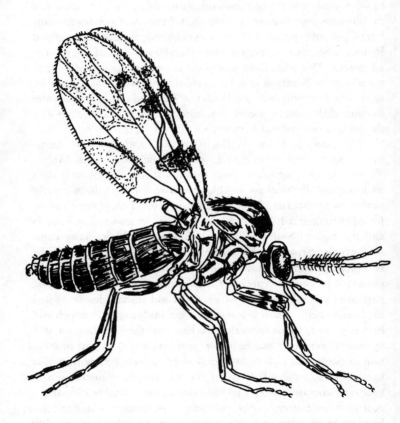

The Highland Midge in flight. Note the characteristic
dark markings on the single pair of wings.

River Kelvin, half a mile from the centre of Glasgow, are a well-known midge-infested haunt in high summer. Midges have not moved into Glasgow; they were there long before Glasgow was built. Midges, indeed, are the most common insect to be found fossilised in amber, some specimens going back almost to the Jurassic, from Canada to Lebanon and Australia, with several indistinguishable from species of midges flying today. Midges were around before mammals and did not become extinct, unlike the dinosaurs on which some may have fed!

WHAT IS A MIDGE?

As members of the Diptera (the two-winged flies), biting midges share several features in common with their relatives the mosquitoes. Biting midges, however, are particularly small with a wingspan of usually less than 2 mm. The Highland Midge is diminutive, with a wingspan of only about 1.4 mm, a feature emphasized by its Gaelic name *meanbh-chuileag* (tiny or pigmy fly) (and hence the oft-heard evening greeting in the Highland summer '*Tha na bugairean dona a-nochd*'!). Any doubts about recognising a biting midge can be quickly settled by looking for the characteristic blotches or dark-flecked spots on the membranous wings. These spots can be readily seen using a low-powered hand-lens and are important, at least to taxonomists, in distinguishing one midge species from another. For example, the distinctive pattern of six to seven separate blotches on the wing of the Highland Midge is quite different from the arrangement of spots on the wing of the Garden Midge. If these dark patches cannot be seen on a living specimen then it is unlikely to be a biting midge. Once seen there is no mistaking them.

Another unusual characteristic of biting midges is the way they fold their wings neatly scissor-like when at rest or when biting and feeding. The generally larger and more obvious dancing midges and related flies usually hold their wings roof-like when at rest. The most likely insect to be confused with the biting midge is the Chironomid or dancing midge. These insects, common in spring, summer and often well into late autumn, are significantly larger than biting midges, they don't bite and are most frequently observed as obvious, often dense, dancing swarms. In these the insects, entirely males, hover backwards and forwards for short distances, but always facing the same direction, usually head into the wind. They will often occupy a favoured site, seemingly for weeks at a time. If these dancing midges are displaced accidentally or deliberately they may get up your nose but they do not bite nor sting. They are unable to; they do not have the right mouth anatomy. Their sole interest in forming these dancing swarms is to attract females for reproduction. Instead they frequently get swatted in mistake for the real culprit, the smaller biting midge. Gatherings of biting midges do occur but they are much less populous and rarely obvious except to the trained eye.

Like other blood-sucking insects, the female biting midge has a well-developed, specialized mouth enabling her both to pierce the skin of her victim as well as to suck up the released blood. Piercing the skin is done by a pair of finely-toothed elongated mandibles and maxillae which work backwards and forwards with a scissor-like action, cutting ever deeper through the skin surface. When the cut or wound is deep enough a pool of blood is released from the fine capillary vessels underlying the skin. At this point the midge quickly rolls her mouth-parts into a fine tube or food-canal which is inserted into the wound to draw up the now free-flowing blood. In mosquitoes and, in all probability, in midges too, saliva is pumped into the wound to prevent the blood from clotting and the flow from drying up. This saliva, with its digestive enzymes, now induces in the victims a mild

The Highland Midge feeding or at rest, with wings
crossed scissor-like over the abdomen.

allergic or immune response causing the victim, human or otherwise, to counter-respond with a rush of histamine to the site of the wound. One of the immediate effects of the histamine is to cause the wounded capillary vessel to stay open for a few minutes to enable the body to mobilize and send in specialized white blood-cells, which in turn set about the task of eliminating any infection and repairing the wound. Those few minutes between breaking into the blood-vessel and the body repairing the wound and staunching the blood-flow are a vital period to the midge. If left undisturbed, the midge will feed for up to 3 or 4 minutes before disengaging. The itching and swelling of the wound area arises directly from the activities of the healthy body's natural repair machinery.

Time, however, may not be on the midge's side. The female midge has to work fast and has evolved her feeding habits to exploit the short time-lag between breaking through the skin and sucking up blood before the blood-vessel closes down. It is a ticklish task for one so small. The male midge on the other hand has a simpler, less specialized, mouth; it doesn't bite animals and probably for that reason has been less studied. It is believed that the males derive all their food-requirements from plant nectar and from rotting plant remains. They are, therefore, of no direct trouble to humans.

BITES AND THE BITING HABIT

One bite from a midge is insignificant, for most people passing unnoticed. However midges rarely work in ones. The evening stimulus for feeding affects large populations of pregnant and hungry females and it is this concerted and simultaneous assault, involving perhaps many hundreds of midges, often concentrated over 20 or 30 minutes, which drives grown men to distraction and to seek shelter or relief from the maddening pursuits of an obsessive but unseen tormentor. Despite this, a number of dedicated scientists have sat it out, and methodically recorded midge bites at the rate of many thousand bites an hour. By this means a fair amount is known about midge biting behaviour.

What it is that attracts a midge to her victim has been the study of recent research in Scotland. Cattle (and probably most mammals) release a complex alcohol, octenol, in their sweat and this, combined with carbon dioxide, acetone, lactic acid and water vapour naturally exhaled in breathing, together acts as a potent cocktail of attractants. In addition, the pregnant female midge releases her own attractant (known from mosquito research as an invitation or recruiting pheromone) which signals to other midges the presence of a suitable victim. This seemingly altruistic open invitation may explain why midges work in large numbers and not singly.

Having first detected her victim mainly by smell (and temperature differences) the midge homes in and attempts to land unnoticed on exposed skin. The final close approach is probably carried out using the insect's eyesight rather than her sense of smell. If the landing is successful the midge will often wander briefly over the surface of the skin, presumably searching for a suitable soft area above a blood-filled capillary before beginning the task of cutting into the epidermis. Sometimes several false or abandoned attempts will be made before a satisfactory wound is secured. So far the victim will have felt little or no pain. If the midge continues to escape attention, some 3 to 4 minutes will be spent feeding on blood.

It is early in this period that the victim becomes first aware of a mildly irritating stinging or pricking sensation, heightened particularly when several midges are biting simultaneously. However, if the midge can secure her meal without interruption she will finally disengage her mouth-parts and retire, fully gorged, for a prolonged rest period. If, as may often happen, feeding is interrupted, then the midge will show her remarkable powers of single-minded obsessive persistence by returning again and again until she has secured her full quota of blood. Less than 0.1 µl (one ten-millionth of a litre) of blood is taken, an insignificantly small amount for the average human adult with about 5.6 litres to spare.

To most people the overall result is no more than a mildly irritating spot, which subsides within a few minutes. But in a small number of susceptible victims the spots may rise to resemble nettle-rash accompanied by a puffiness of the affected area, particularly if the bites are on the forehead, eyelid and lips. How each person responds depends, in part, on how often he or she has been exposed to midge bites before. For first-time visitors to the Highlands the response to being bitten is minimal, this blissful state of innocence lasting perhaps for three to four days. These lucky souls have an immune system which has not yet been triggered to respond to midge bites, or more probably to certain proteins in the midge saliva. Because they have no specific antibodies with which to recognize midge saliva, the bite has no noticeable effect. But, unfortunately, this state of purity has to end; with increasing exposure to attacks, the body's immune system kicks in.

Coursing through the bloodstream are white cells which form specific anti-midge antibodies and which for ever more will recognize the foreign proteins in midge saliva and will go on to trigger an immediate response to any similar midge bites in the future. So, on the next occasion when midges attack, there is a rapid mobilization of the defence and repair mechanisms that exist in every healthy person, which lead to the destruction of the midge saliva contents and make repairs to the wound. The natural and healthy response of the immune system is also to pump histamine into the site of the fresh wound to prepare the way for the protective work to be done by the white blood-cells. The result is a wound which is perhaps slightly swollen and red, perhaps a little itchy, but rapidly undergoing repair and where the midge saliva is promptly detoxified. All very healthy. However, the price to be paid for all this healthy and fast-acting self-protection is that the victim is left with a mildly uncomfortable to slightly irritating spot, the irritation lasting for some few minutes. Most people, visitors after a few days and locals alike, respond in this way, given reasonably good health. A very few people, however, over-respond by becoming quite ill and may need to seek prompt medical attention. Their immune responses are rather too active. However, these unfortunate souls are usually well aware of their condition, often because they know that their bodies over-react to bites or stings from other kinds of insects. There is some evidence that high concentrations of vitamin B1 taken over a period of more than 30 days before exposure to midges may reduce the severity of some people's over-reaction to bites. Others claim similar effects from a high dose of brewer's yeast.

Among the local population, including long-term settlers, many individuals, but by no means all, develop with age a much more controlled, slower and less severe reaction to midge bites. These are the fortunate, seemingly enviable crofters who appear to escape the attention of the midges. They don't at all. It is only that with years of exposure to midge bites their immune system may become rather slow to respond. Bee-keepers with years of experience similarly show a sluggish response when they are stung by bees. However, if it is any consolation there are a great many Highlanders, perhaps the majority, who to their dying day suffer just as much as the tourist after the first week of a holiday in the area. The difference, however, is that these Highlanders have a knack of predicting when and where the midges are going to be out. Forewarned, they know what to do to avoid the worst of the attacks.

WHEN AND WHY DO MIDGES BITE?

Seasonally, in Scotland, several midge species are active from April until October. These early and late-season fliers are rarely of much trouble to humans. The Highland Midge, *C. impunctatus*, first appears on the wing at the start of June, though in recent years the warmer temperatures in spring may account for the trend of midges appearing as early as the middle of May in some years. However, most of this early hatch are non-biting males who have no interest in molesting humans. The first serious biting episodes really begin in early to mid-June and persist to varying degrees of severity throughout July and into August. The height of the biting season lasts for about 12 weeks. Towards the end of August midge numbers decline rapidly, just as many tourists turn south. By mid-September the midges are no longer an intolerable problem. The attacks are less prolonged and rarely more than a slight nuisance, although in some years, given a mild and wet late summer, there may be one or two last-ditch assaults until the end of the month. The Garden Midge, *C. obsoletus*, lingers on into October in towns and sheltered coastal areas. Its bite is generally much less irritating.

For most people, from September until the following June, the midges can be quietly forgotten, allowing the Highlands to be enjoyed to their full. Seasoned visitors to Scotland know that the Highlands are often at their best before June and after August; then the visitors can enjoy their hard-earned holiday without fear of a bite. For those who have little choice but to visit during the summer months there is still much that can be done to avoid at least the worst effects of the attacks.

Few midges, in Britain, are active biters throughout the daylight hours. The aptly-named *C. heliophilus* (sun-lover) is an exception and prefers to bite around high noon. It is, however, much less common than the Highland Midge. Like most of the

18

Scottish species, the Highland Midge is particularly sensitive to light and, depending on weather conditions, bites most vigorously towards the long evening twilight or in the first hour or two of dawn. The first stimulus for biting in this species occurs towards dusk as the radiation from the sun declines to below 260 Watts/m^2. (Putting this into perspective, full sunlight in north Scotland on a cloudless noon in midsummer gives about 800 Watts/m^2, way over the threshold at which midges bite). As the sun's radiation decreases and the light fades, so midge activity begins. And as the sun's radiation declines further to about 130 Watts/m^2, as happens at sunset on a cloudless midsummer evening, this is the trigger for clouds of midges to rise from the ground cover, such as heather and bracken, on which they have been sheltering. The same process in reverse takes place at around dawn, as many a camper will know. Taking the height of the holiday season as the last two weeks of July and the first week of August, midge activity at dawn, on a cloudless day, rockets from about 5 o'clock in the morning, peaks around 7 o'clock, and falls to relatively low numbers by 8—all the time midge activity tracks the radiation from the sun up through the critical 260 Watts/m^2 barrier. At times this dawn assault may exceed the ferocity of the evening attack.

What often puzzles people is why midges go on to bite during the day. The explanation is that high unbroken cloud, even at midday, can reduce the radiation from the sun to below the critical 260 Watts/m^2. Thick low grey-white clouds will take the radiation down to even lower levels, as will dark rain–clouds. It is this dull cloudy weather which brings the midges out to bite in the morning or afternoon. In the forests, even on a cloudless day, the deep shade stimulates midges to bite for most of the daylight hours.

The apparent association of midges with warm humid weather is more to do with the cloud cover and lack of wind than humidity itself. Midges will bite avidly on dry evenings as the sun goes

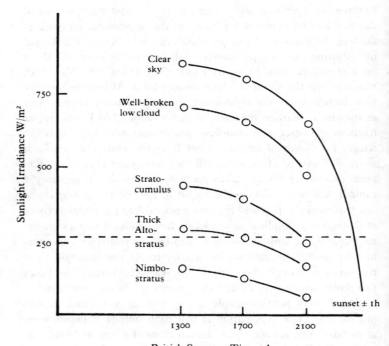

Sunlight irradiance through various types of cloud in the course of a mid-summer afternoon and evening in Scotland (latitude 60° N). The sunlight penetration is reduced by thick and low clouds and when it declines to below 260 W/m² , this is the threshold for the Highland Midge to bite.

WHEN AND WHY DO MIDGES BITE?

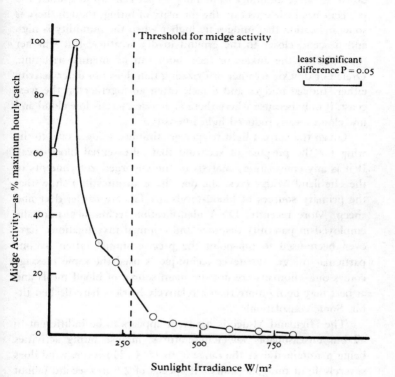

Flying activity of the Highland Midge in relation to sunlight irradiance. Above 260 W/m², sunlight suppresses midge activity. At about 100 to 130 W/m², midge numbers and biting reach their maximum.

down. Relative humidity from a dry 65 per cent up to a moist 100 per cent has little effect on the intensity of biting, though there is some indication that midges fly higher when the humidity is high and descend closer to the ground in dry weather. But whether they bite on the ankles or face, both can be mighty irritating. Dreich or drackie weather or drizzling rain does not deter activity either. Indeed midges and drizzle often go together on the west coast, if only because where there is drizzle there is low cloud and low cloud means reduced light intensity.

Given the correct light trigger or stimulus, midges take to the wing for the purpose of securing that all-essential blood-meal. If it is any consolation, analysis of the engorged gut contents of the Highland Midge (yes, she does have an intestine) show that the primary sources of blood-meals, by far, are cattle, deer and sheep. More recently, DNA identification techniques, normally employed in paternity disputes and criminal investigations, have even been used to pin-point the precise animal bitten by one particular midge. Whatever technique is used the same message comes out—humans are not the main source of blood-meals and at best may be no more than a relatively hairless bare-fleshed tit-bit. Some consolation!

The Highland Midge is hardy; it appears to be indifferent to all but unseasonably low temperatures, intense biting activities being maintained over the range 8° to 18° C. However, wind does severely limit midge assaults. At speeds of 2.5 m./second (about 5.5 mph), that is up to a slight breeze, midge biting continues unabated. But above this wind-speed they are forced to seek shelter, usually on ground vegetation or, where available, on dark-coloured tree-trunks. Young conifer plantations, bracken and thick unburned heather appear to offer suitable sanctuary from the wind. But once the wind passes and calm airs prevail, clouds of midges can be seen rising in unison, anxious to get on with the task of securing a meal.

Taking all environmental components into account, the most important single factor which immediately determines the intensity of the biting activity is light. Cloudless days and the midges will not stir until sunset. Dark rain-clouds and the midges are out in the middle of the day. In good summers, however, it is the prolonged evening and dawn twilight around midsummer which offers an ideal environment for the Highland Midge. From mid-May until the end of July, twilight, at least the nautical definition of twilight, lasts throughout the night in mid-Scotland (latitude 56°N). It is no surprise, at least to experienced campers, to find that midges can and frequently do continue biting into the small hours, and again before dawn. Midge activity is suppressed by bright light but triggered by dim light. Whip open the curtains late in the evening and look at the midges baying to get in at the window!

Alison Blackwell, working in Argyll, recorded the flying activity of the Highland Midge hour by hour, night and day, for nearly three weeks at the height of the season. She found that peak activity occurred between 5 and 6 o'clock in the morning and between 9 and 11 o'clock in the evening. Most of the midges caught were unfed females, carrying their second batch of eggs and foraging for a blood meal. Activity in both periods was heightened in damp, windless and warm weather.

OTHER BITING INSECTS

Not every insect that bites in a summer evening is a midge. In Scotland there are other groups of flying blood-suckers, the mosquito, stable fly, black fly and the notorious cleg, gleg or horse fly. All are much larger than midges. In addition there is an unrelated collection of rather more personalized biters, the fleas, lice, bed-bugs and ticks: perhaps less visible, but all too obvious when active. There are other biting insects in Scotland but for most people they are not common. The account which follows is, then, a very brief summary of the most common Scottish biters likely to be met in midge country and whose bite could be mistaken for that of a midge.

It surprises many people to learn that mosquitoes are to be found in Scotland, though perhaps not in the numbers of their smaller cousins. Of the thirty or so species of mosquito in the British Isles, all are several times larger than a midge. These two-winged, delicate, long-legged insects have a wingspan of about 4 to 5 mm (say ¼ inch), often with colourful iridescent or at least bicoloured bodies. Like the midge, only the female hunts for blood before developing her eggs. Unlike midges, however, most mosquitoes lay their eggs on or close to water, though this need for water can be met by puddles, rain-water butts or gutters on houses. In Scotland there are four groups of mosquitoes—those that persistently inhabit buildings, those breeding in woodlands, those found on the sea-shore or on coastal marshes and, fourthly, those of the field and moorland.

Predictably, those mosquitoes that share human dwellings or outbuildings are the most readily seen in Scotland. Often known as house-gnats, these mosquitoes fly from April through to October. One, *Culex pipiens*, seems to be increasing in numbers in recent years, possibly as a consequence of the recent run of warmer summers. Those species which are able to hibernate over winter may give the odd midwinter nip if disturbed. One member of this group of household mosquitoes was responsible for the malaria, or ague as it was known, that persisted in the fenlands of east England up to the 1850s and in north Kent up to the 1920s. Migrant farm labourers from the Lothians took the ague back home from Essex every autumn. Fortunately, malaria today, in Britain, is extremely rare. Despite their harmlessness, the female mosquitoes continue to inflict a painful bite, mostly at night and often when the victim is asleep. These house mosquitoes are readily recognized by their high-pitched piping or singing, particularly when flying close to the ear.

The forest-dwelling mosquitoes are, perhaps, less often met with; they tend to bite only near their breeding sites. The coastal species, sometimes found on shore-line seaweed, can be vicious and persistent biters. Perhaps the most common mosquito outwith buildings and away from the seashore is one with the name *Aedes punctor*, characteristic of moorlands, heath, birch and pine forests. This common Scottish species lays its eggs in dry holes or depressions that fill up with water in winter. The adult female is particularly persistent in her attacks when a suitable bloodmeal moves into her breeding grounds. Fortunately mosquitoes in this country probably no longer transmit diseases; they are merely irritating, some species giving a painful bite which may form a blister. On the west coast, mosquitoes are, at worst, a minor nuisance.

A quite different biter is the black fly. This short-legged plump black insect with a wing-span of about 5 mm is a scourge of Man in parts of northern Canada and Siberia. In several parts of Africa and Arabia these flies carry tropical diseases. In the British Isles one of the twenty native species is all too familiar for its unpleasant habit of feeding on the inside of horses' ears. At times they can cause considerable distress in stables. A related species of black fly is fairly common in the Scottish Lowlands and is also known from Strathspey where it will attack humans with a persistence which can be infuriating in the extreme. Once again, as with midges and mosquitoes, it is the female which does all the biting. The size of the insect, so much larger than a midge, makes its attention all too obvious.

For stealth, the cleg, gleg or horse fly takes the prize. It flies in complete silence, and alights so gently on its victim, whether horse, cow or human, to make a painless incision in the flesh before slipping its mouth parts into the wound. The stoutly-built,

sombre, dusky-grey female, with large bulging eyes, usually working singly, will even bite through clothing or hair. Left undisturbed, with its head down and tail cocked up, it will feed for one
or two minutes. It has the audacity to make a second wound nearby if the first proves unsatisfactory. The pain comes the moment
feeding is over, and the cleg has left the scene. The bite shows as
a faint red ring which can persist and remain irritable for several
days and often develops with a distinct swelling around the bitten area. Clegs, unlike midges and many mosquitoes, feed mainly
during warm bright days and, in Scotland at least, are less active
in cool, cloudy weather. In the Highlands they are only common
in July and August. Clegs, mosquitoes and midges do share one
feature in common in their attraction to dark-coloured clothing,
particularly when the wearer is perspiring profusely. Perhaps they
have a taste for ministers!

Scotland also has biters related to the African tse-tse fly. Known
here as the stable fly, it is similar in appearance to the common
house fly. Both males and females will attack horses, cattle and, on
occasions, humans. At times their numbers can reach intolerable
proportions. The eggs are laid on decaying plant matter, particularly wet, soiled, animal bedding which has been allowed to accumulate in byres and stables. Persistent outbreaks of large populations
of stable flies are often a sign of poor animal hygiene.

Bed-bugs, certain lice and fleas have long enjoyed human com-
pany. In these days of improved personal hygiene these parasites are much less common than in previous centuries. However,
in times of natural disasters, such as earthquakes or hurricanes,
where access to washing facilities or a change of clothing becomes
difficult, so these creatures multiply, bringing with them outbreaks
of typhus and, in times past, bubonic plague. Today, for most people, their presence is harmless and at best an overnight irritant.

A more obvious irritant, particularly to bare-legged hill
walkers, is the tick family. More closely related to spiders than

insects, these round-bodied pale grey, light brown to black parasites lock themselves on to tall grasses, bracken or heather waiting for a bare leg or arm to brush past. On making physical contact with its new-found host, the tick moves fast over the skin to nuzzle in on a suitable warm site like the back of the knee, neck or armpit where it proceeds to cut its way through the skin to sink its head painlessly into the victim's flesh. There, if left undisturbed, it will cement itself into position and hang for days, its soft body swelling to a considerable size with blood before dropping off fully gorged. Young ticks in the larval or nymph stage of development are much the most common, and being no more than pinhead sized or less, may be difficult to spot, particularly when they work their way into soft folds of the body. The less common adults may be two to three mm in size or more, and are unlikely to be missed. Ticks should not be left feeding but should be removed at an early opportunity. The only safe way to remove ticks is with a pair of tweezers, held at the skin surface and pulled, gently but firmly, straight out (pulled not twisted). If they are carelessly removed the barbed headpiece may be left in the skin and so introduce infection. If tweezers are not immediately available it is probably better to leave the tick undisturbed for a few hours until tweezers can be obtained. Certainly it is not advisable to try to dig out the tick with a needle or finger nails. Application of vaseline, soap, whisky (applied to the tick), burning matches or lighter flames do not work and will rarely encourage the tick to release its hold. More likely the tick will be forced to squirt back its gut contents into the wound, so increasing the risk of infection. As with their cousins on the continent and North America, the all-too-common sheep tick of Europe, including Scotland, may carry Lyme disease and should not be ignored. Medical advice should be sought where a tick bite leaves a persistent and spreading red weal or rash. Chronic Lyme disease can, with time, affect the joints, heart and central nervous system.

Lyme disease is present in Britain from Dorset in the south to the outer isles in the north, and probably has been for many decades, though largely unrecognized as a tick-borne malady. Increasingly, medical practitioners are becoming familiar with the symptoms of Lyme disease and are able to offer effective antibiotics to counter the bacteria causing the infection. But again, to put this firmly into perspective, crofters and keepers who work with sheep and deer are regularly exposed to ticks and have long learned to watch for bites that do not clear up promptly. Experienced walkers and campers make a whole body check for ticks each evening and remove any they find. Most residents in the Highlands come across ticks on themselves, their children and household pets throughout the season from March to October and, increasingly, into November.

As a further point of reassurance, most Scottish sheep ticks do not harbour the organism causing Lyme disease, but even if the Lyme disease bacterium is present, provided the tick is removed within a day, the risk of infection is minimal. The Scottish Highlands are not particularly notorious for ticks and Lyme disease—there is probably more risk of catching Lyme disease in Bavaria, the pasture lands of Southern Sweden or even the English New Forest.

While Man has his share of annoyance from biting flies, his farm animals, deer, rabbits and birds appear to have more than their fair share. Apart from horse and stable flies, many large animals suffer the almost constant attention of ticks, warble flies, several species of black flies as well as mosquitoes and, invariably in Scotland, several kinds of midge. Although veterinary science has helped to reduce the scourge of warble and ticks in cattle, wild deer continue to suffer fierce attacks. Rabbits have their fleas, the vector for the myxomatosis virus.

There is some good news in this unpleasant story, at least for humans. For most people, away from byres, poultry sheds or stables, many of these biting creatures are not common. Most are readily dissuaded from attacking humans by the application of products marketed as insect repellents. For most people by far the most frequent biter in Scotland, particularly in the west and north, is the midge. With the possible exception of the Highland Midge, the cleg and perhaps one or two species of mosquito, most flying blood-sucking insects and ticks show a marked, almost exclusive, preference for cattle, sheep, deer or birds. Only when disturbed from their natural or preferred host will they take on humans. So most summer visitors to the Highlands will rarely experience the attention of stable flies or black flies, although almost certainly a mosquito or two will make an evening attack. Visitors from the south, however, will experience far more bites from mosquitoes back at home. The average English cottage garden has quite a collection of mosquitoes and no holiday in Italy is complete without a fair number of mosquito bites. American visitors may be relieved to see the back of their own mosquito population, though they may not be too enamoured with the Scottish midge. Clegs are occasionally a nuisance for perhaps two months of high summer in Scotland, but in south Germany and parts of France they are active biters from April to the end of October.

It may be also worth reminding ourselves of what many emigrant Highland families experienced when they landed on the shores of Nova Scotia two hundred years ago. They may have thought fondly that they had finally seen the back of the midges of Scotland. But when the first pioneering families landed near Pictou they had to contend not only with dispossessed Indians and resentful French settlers, but found themselves hunted mercilessly by mosquitoes pouring out of the forests around their landfall. Today those Nova Scotian mosquitoes spend the summer tormenting the tourists in the many otherwise idyllic campsites.

To put all this into context, many biting insects that are common in Europe, in England and North America have their counterpart in Scotland, but in most cases in relatively low numbers. The distinctive ecology of the Highlands, the climate, the prolonged twilight and particularly the high rainfall have tilted the balance in favour of just one group of biters, the midges. The rest of the biting insects seem to be, at times, almost a welcome conversational diversion.

BITING AND DISEASE

Many important diseases are harboured and transmitted by biting insects, particularly in the tropics. These include malaria and yellow fever by several species of mosquitoes, sleeping sickness by tse-tse flies and river blindness by blackflies. Concern about the role of midges as carriers of disease is natural and their role in disease transmission has been studied by scientists, medical entomologists and veterinary surgeons for many years.

The concerns begin with the feeding habits of midges. The majority of biting midge species, including those in Scotland, feed on more than one host. The most commonly recorded victims are domesticated animals, many wild animals including deer, rabbits and wild birds and, way down the list, humans. While subjectively it may seem that both the Highland and the Garden Midge prefer to attack humans, both of these species feed largely on cattle, horses, sheep and deer. In terms of disease transmission to humans, the Scottish midges are, as far as we know, harmless. Several species do, however cause extreme misery to horses, sheep and cattle. Deer herds in Scotland, Russia and North America have been recorded as being driven out of low-lying pastures by increased midge activity and forced on to the impoverished slopes of the high hills. Midges may be one of the reasons why, until recent years, the Scottish red deer was an ill-fed and poorly developed specimen compared with its European cousins.

Midges have long been blamed for distress in cows, and in bad midgy summers may be responsible for declines in milk-yields. Horses suffer greatly; a number of unpleasant equine disorders, such as sweet itch and fistulous withers are known to be caused by several species of midge. Some of these midge species show a marked preference for biting particular areas of the mane, belly or flank, and persist again and again in feeding from the same wound, causing considerable distress to the animal. Much more serious, however, are the potentially lethal midge-borne diseases found on the continent of Europe and overseas, particularly in the sub-tropics and tropics. There, several midge species transmit a number of economically important viral, protozoan and micro-filarial diseases to sheep, cattle and horses as well as to the indigenous wild animals. In recent years a number of outbreaks of these diseases have resulted in considerable losses to the farming communities in these countries and have provoked active veterinary research in the United States, parts of Africa, central America and in Australia. Outbreaks of an important midge-borne disease of ruminants, blue tongue virus (BTV), finally reached East Anglia in the summer of 2007, after years spreading north on the Continent. Affecting the mouth and nasal passage, the virus causes fever and muscle weakness and can be fatal if untreated. Immediate restriction on cattle movements and introduction of a vaccine the following year successfully brought the outbreak under control. The vector was a species of midge, possibly *C. obsoletus* or a close relative, though other midge species could be implicated, at least on the basis of laboratory-based studies. By 2008, vaccination, compulsory or voluntary, was in place throughout the EU countries affected, and no further cases were reported from Britain. However, given the concern over the possible reappearance of BTV, the Institute of Animal Health has provided a website, *www.culicoides.net*, as an information bank for farmers, crofters, vets and public. In Scotland, despite the availability of a vaccine, warnings remain over the import of animals from affected parts of Europe, particularly at times of the year when adult midges are present. It took just a single shipment of Namibian zebras into Spain to introduce African horse sickness virus (*C. obsoletus* is a known carrier) with lethal consequences for the Andalusian horse bloodstock.

Cross-border movement of breeding stock and animals for slaughter within the EU, combined with more favourable climates, are likely to pull more midge-borne diseases northwards. Parallels are being drawn with tick-borne diseases of cattle, sheep and pigs, which have spread from Mediterranean countries and eastwards from the former Soviet Union in recent years. The warnings are there.

Art Borkent and Doug Kettle (see bibliography) have provided a compendium of known midge-borne diseases, viral, protozoan and filarial. Affected hosts include most wild and domesticated animals, birds, monkeys, rodents and kangaroos, through to humans. With the exception of a few debilitating disorders largely confined to the Caribbean and Central America, humans get off lightly, however. Over the years midges have time and again been suspected of transmitting diseases to humans but, on investigation, have usually emerged with a clean ticket. More recently there has been speculation that midges and their cousins, mosquitoes, might transmit the AIDS viruses. Several authorities have examined this, but the consensus, particularly for mosquitoes, is that the virus cannot survive within an insect, let alone be transmitted by one. The reality is AIDS or the antibodies to the virus are largely confined to sexually active adults and, with well-explained exceptions, are not found in children nor in the very elderly. Yet midges and mosquitoes bite the young, middle-aged and old, male and female, without discrimination. In other words, the incidence of AIDS bears no resemblance to the biting behaviour and host preferences of midges.

None of these assurances, and none of these comments about midges being more dangerous overseas, are intended to diminish in any way the undoubted and unqualified distress that midges can cause to humans during the summer months in Scotland. The Scottish Highlands are fortunate in not having the insect-borne diseases that afflict many warmer countries. Instead, Scotland holds enormous populations of midges and it is their immense number and their single focus on getting to blood that makes the midge problem so acute here. There can be few more sobering sights than young women on their first camping holiday in the Highlands crying in the public toilets in Glencoe at five in the morning, trying to shelter from the midge pack outside. That is real distress.

LIFE CYCLE—THE KEY TO SUCCESS

One of the reasons for the success of midges in Scotland is their unusual life-pattern, which has evolved to become well-adapted to the Scottish environment, particularly the weather. Like most insects, the midge undergoes several distinct stages of development, from egg to larva, larva to pupa, before emerging as the familiar flying adult. However, with midges, the egg and pupal stages are unusually short, generally lasting only for a few days.

It is the larval stage which dominates in midge life cycles. Up to 10 months is spent as a small maggot or caterpillar-like larva. And each species of midge has its own distinct or preferred habitat for its larva. While some species develop on the surface of the muddy margins of inland lochs, others exploit sea-coast marshes or damp areas in farmyards or drainage ditches. The Highland Midge larva grows from an egg on the moist blanket bogs, raised mires and poorly drained acidic grasslands that cover much of upland Britain, particularly in the wetter areas of the west. A

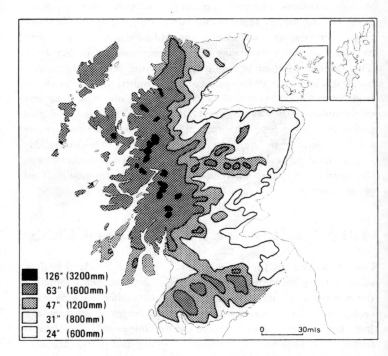

126" (3200 mm)
63" (1600 mm)
47" (1200 mm)
31" (800 mm)
24" (600 mm)

0   30 mls

Average annual rainfall in Scotland. The Highland Midge
is found predominantly in the areas of the west and north
where rainfall exceeds 50 inches (1,250 mm) a year.

suitable breeding site, for this species, is one which is relatively moist throughout the winter and summer but is reasonably free of standing water. Such sites are often marked by the presence of *Sphagnum* and *Polytrichum* mosses, particularly where there is some groundwater movement from the presence of nearby burns and ditches. To the botanist, the jointed rush *Juncus articulatus* and sharp-flowered rush *J. acutiflorus* and the presence of sphagnum mosses are a good indicator of the larval breeding grounds of the Highland Midge. Just such sites are widespread throughout much of the west and central Highlands and Hebrides. With some 4 million hectares at hand it is hardly surprising that enormous populations of midges can exist. Estimates of up to 24 million midge larvae per hectare (10 million per acre) have been made. It is likely that even these numbers are exceeded in the damp, not too acidic soils of the coastal straths of the north and west Highlands. The dauntless Alison Blackwell once trapped an estimated 500,000 midges emerging from just one 2x2m square area on the Ormsary Estate in Argyll.

In whatever habitat the eggs are laid, a critical aspect of midge survival is the need for moisture. Both the larvae and pupae are susceptible to desiccation. A dry spring and early summer can spell disaster for the new generation of midges, but for humans and livestock it can serve as a forecast of a relatively midge-free season. A wet spring, however, usually means a midgy summer. West of meridian 4°30′, within 60 km of the Atlantic seaboard, the average annual rainfall exceeds 1,250 mm (50 inches) and in some places regularly exceeds 2,500 mm (100 inches). These high-rainfall areas in the west of Scotland are the heart of the midge country. In the drier east, midges become less of a problem. Much of the east coast up to Aberdeenshire is comparatively free of midges, though there are years when even the hardy Aberdonians suffer. Given the right habitat and sufficient rainfall, midges will flourish by the millions.

The breeding cycle begins when the eggs are laid during the thirteen weeks of summer. In the case of the Highland Midge, the eggs are deposited three to five days after fertilization in batches of fifty or more, probably on the surface of saturated humus or on wet vegetation on the soil surface. Within a day or two, perhaps a week or so in colder weather, the hatching larvae burrow into the top 2 to 3 cm of soil, migrating a little deeper during daylight hours or when the soil surface dries out. There they develop slowly through four stages, to mature, after Christmas, as small, 5 mm-long, opaque-white caterpillars or maggots. While buried, the larvae acquire a voracious appetite and, during the ten months or so spent underground as a larva, the body-length increases some six-fold. Capable of limited motion, the omnivorous midge larvae rove through the moist soil feeding on a wide range of other larvae, nematodes, protozoa, green algae and, presumably, a wide selection of fungal spores and mycelia. Some species are not above a little cannibalism given the opportunity. When fully grown, and with increasing day-length and warmer temperatures from mid-May to July, the larvae develop into the non-feeding pupal stage close to the surface of the soil. In some species, the pupae are capable of a flicking movement, probably to counter the effects of desiccation. This is a key moment in the life cycle. A prolonged drought at this critical stage can have a profound effect on the number of adults which finally emerge in the succeeding days. Good or bad midge-seasons, at least from a human viewpoint, will often depend on the rainfall in June and July as the pupae develop and mature. Prolonged dry weather has been shown to reduce populations of the Highland Midge by 90 per cent or more. Good midge-free days during summer can often be traced back to a dry spell two or three weeks earlier which may have wiped out large numbers of moisture-sensitive pupae.

The first adults to fly, from mid-May, seem to be predominantly male. They form gatherings of all-male swarms, usually at

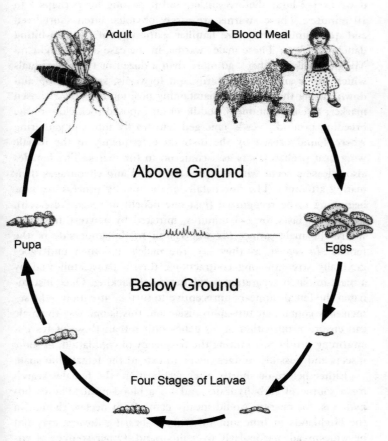

Above Ground

Below Ground

Adult

Blood Meal

Eggs

Pupa

Four Stages of Larvae

Life cycle of the Highland Midge over 12 months
(drawing by Ishy Hendry).

dawn or 1-2 hours before sunset, and persisting for perhaps 5 to 10 minutes. These swarms are rarely obvious, often short-lived and quite unlike the more familiar gatherings of the non-biting dancing midges. These male swarms, in the case of the Highland Midge, involve perhaps no more than a dozen or two individuals which hover and fly backwards and forwards, spiralling up and down, facing the wind and maintaining position over their chosen marker, often a prominent puddle or an exposed rock close to the breeding ground. Newly emerged females fly into the gathering where sound caused by the distinctive frequency of the female wing beat probably acts as a come-on to the males. The females also release a scent which excites the males and encourages their mating attempts. The fine details of the mating process are now beginning to be recognized (just one benefit of recent research). Copulation lasts for 2-3 minutes, initiated by a wrestling phase where the male gropes his way round to the underside of the female. *In copula,* as they say, the male's abdomen undergoes gradually strengthening contractions, then a pause, followed by a male-initiated separation involving much kicking. Once inseminated the female appears unreceptive to further attention—the semen may contain an anti-aphrodisiac and this is one way the male can ensure propagation of *his* genes rather than those of his co-swarming brothers. Limiting the frequency of copulation, in some insects and possibly midges, helps to extend the female life span.

Either before or shortly after fertilization, the females search for a source of carbohydrates and for a blood-meal. The carbohydrates, for energy, would ideally come from nectar, though in the Highlands in June and July, nectar-bearing flowers may not be widespread, particularly over moorland. Other sources of energy are sought and may include sap-wounds from trees and rotting vegetation. But the critical step for the females is to secure a supply of fresh blood. For most midge species this is a key moment in reproduction; without it egg development is arrested and, given the short life-span of twenty, perhaps thirty, days for the adult, this is the point on which all future generations depend absolutely.

So much is true for the greater majority of biting midge species in Scotland. However, the Highland Midge has one trick up its diminutive sleeve. Blood-meals are also none too common in the Highlands. Ranging across the hills, glens and straths, large, warm-blooded mammals, humans included, can be rare or even non-existent to an insect with a limited flight-range. However, the Highland Midge, unlike many other species of midge, has partly solved this problem. It has evolved a way of maturing and laying at least some of its first batch of eggs without a blood-meal. Whether it sacrifices part of its flight-muscle, which carries a similar nutrient to blood, in order to mature the eggs is not known for certain, but is a possibility. This process of maturing even a few eggs in the absence of a blood-meal (known as autogeny) is perhaps central to the peculiar success of the Highland Midge. At least it ensures that there will be some survivors for next year. To develop further egg-batches, however, a blood-meal is absolutely essential for this species. It is these females, having given birth once autogenously, which now form much the bulk of the biting population. For good reason they are obsessive in their pursuit of blood.

Eventually, perhaps, a blood-meal is secured and at this point the females disappear (at least from the collecting records). Although it is not known for certain, it seems most likely that these well-fed females seek cover and rest in long grass, heather or on nearby tree trunks where they quickly lose the urge for further biting. They no longer react to the evening or dawn stimulus to attack. Over the course of the next few days, the eggs mature to be laid, as before, in a suitable damp breeding site. These eggs now represent the major part of the new generation which will emerge as flying adults the following year. Recent research,

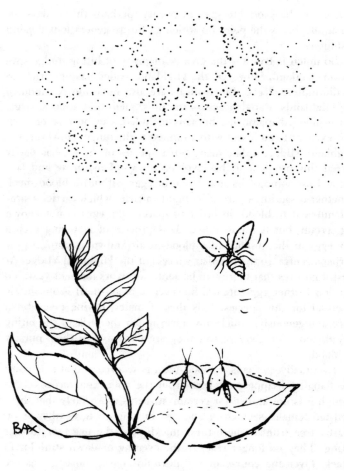

FANCY HER GOING DRINKING
AND DANCING IN HER CONDITION.

however, has confirmed that eggs laid early enough in the summer may develop, given adequate rainfall and warm enough temperatures, through the larval and pupal stages very rapidly indeed, over a matter of weeks, to emerge as a late summer flush of new adults just in time for the start of the grouse and deer shooting season. It is possible that this second generation may assume greater significance in the event of warmer summer temperatures under future climates.

FLIGHT RANGE

In open country, over grassland and moorland, midges will drift passively for considerable distances, particularly in continuous light breezes. Under the right conditions in summer, large populations can be carried a kilometre or more from the larval breeding grounds. Some hapless specimens have even been trapped many miles from land out in the North Sea. Others have been caught at considerable altitudes, from aircraft, in rising warm air-currents. The appearance of midges on some of the smaller west coast islands otherwise unsuited to midge breeding, such as Iona, Staffa and the Shiant Isles, may be due to drifting from the neighbouring mainland. This long-distance passive movement of midges in light winds is one important reason why chemical control through spraying of larvicide on to midge breeding grounds is largely ineffective in Scotland. It makes no sense to attempt to treat the open grounds surrounding, say, an isolated Highland hotel or caravan site when a nearby population of hungry females will be blown in on the next favourable light breeze. Yet there have been examples in recent years of money being spent in futile attempts to provide an imagined *cordon sanitaire* round high-value sites.

In sheltered locations, particularly in established woodlands and in maturing forestry plantations, the adult midge population does not readily disperse far from the breeding grounds. Woodlands in the Highlands are often notoriously midgy, partly because of the reduced light from shading trees and partly because the still air in forests does not promote passive dispersal. Because of this, the intensity of biting in a plantation is usually directly related to the nearness of the victim to the actual breeding grounds. The author once gave an interview for the BBC Natural History programme in a Highland woodland and, quite unintentionally, almost on top of a midge breeding site. The recording lasted for less than two minutes before the interviewer pulled the plug and fled from the site. The immediacy and vitality of those dying seconds of the interview won it a place in the natural history recording annals!

Away from sheltered sites, midge intensity diminishes with elevation. Just as red deer seek relief from midges by moving to higher altitudes, so hill-walkers know that it is possible to avoid midge molestation on hillsides by climbing ever higher. Indeed the relief to be gained from reaching an exposed windy site may be one good reason for driving the tired walker onwards to the summit. It is the prospect of a midgy night in the still air of the camp site down in the glen which spoils the idyll.

THE IMPACT OF MIDGES ON THE HIGHLAND ECONOMY

The appearance of biting midges from late May to late August can be relied upon with confidence. Inevitably, this twelve to thirteen week period coincides with particular activities or seasonal cycles in the Highland calendar. To the farmer and crofter in the west Highlands, this period is usually given over to the single hay crop and hay-drying and to sheep-shearing. The greater impact comes from tourism, with the economy of the Highlands centred

LOOK, MORAG—
A FOOD
CHAIN

on hotels, b&bs, self-catering houses, caravan sites, craft shops, castles and museums. As autumn starts at the end of August, with snows falling as early as September or October, Highland livings now depend on lamb sales, fishing, fish-farming and forestry.

Given that the three months of summer can play such a significant part in local livelihoods, it is surprising to find that little has been published on the impact of midges on the Highland economy. Market research and consumer surveys certainly have been conducted from time to time, some on behalf of Visit-Scotland or its predecessors, but their findings have remained confidential. More accessible have been the several independent university-funded surveys carried out among tourists, usually as part of the justification for research funding. One survey round Loch Awe conducted over several weeks predictably showed that the majority of visitors staying in purpose-built log cabins had been adversely affected by midges and that the experience had put them off from coming back to that particular site, at that time of year. Another more recent independent survey, carried out by Alison Blackwell of Edinburgh University, among tourists in camp-sites, bed and breakfast accommodation and youth hostels, indicated that two-thirds of the visitors felt that the midges (and this *was* the height of the midge season) had put them off from returning to Scotland at that particular time of the year. An even higher percentage of first-time visitors were prepared to warn off their friends and family from coming on holiday to the Highlands. Among the recreational pursuits most affected by midges were walking, horse riding, eating *al fresco*, camping, golf and—heartfelt cries here—simply being outside early in the morning! Being unable to open windows on warm summer evenings was not viewed kindly. The message from this and other surveys is that many tourists have had distressing experiences with midges, deterring some from returning to the Highlands in future summers. In fairness it should be added that poor weather in summer, particularly rainy days, can fuel discontent, with or without midges.

Apart from the opinions of tourists there are numerous hearsay stories about the impact of midges on the Highland economy and culture. One that can be substantiated is the effect of midges on the traditional Highland game of shinty. This age-old celtic ball game, formerly played in autumn and winter, is now played throughout the spring and summer, right through the midge season. While so far there are no records of summer shinty matches actually being abandoned, evening games fought out among clouds of midges are extremely unpopular among players and spectators, and the resulting bad language, off and on the field of play, usually has little to do with the quality of refereeing! Midges have also been credited with interfering with a rather different aspect of culture, that of drama. Out on Rannoch Moor recently, some ill-advised souls had to abandon attempts to perform an open-air production of Shakespeare's *The Tempest*. Calls of deep distress were also heard from the cast and crew filming the BBC Highland drama *Monarch of the Glen* on the bonny, bonny banks of Loch Laggan.

Despite the surveys and hoary tales of midge-attacks, the truth is that tourists, shooters, game-fishers and their families flock to the Highlands in summer and autumn. Complaining about midges is part of the whole Highland experience. Look at the jokey postcards on sale about midges (sheep and kilts). Hotel-keepers do grouse about cancellations following a sequence of prolonged midgy evenings, though no doubt they benefit from the midge-bitten walker seeking relief in the hotel bar. The Highland restaurant trade, particularly at the quality end of the market, has enjoyed international acclaim, midges or no.

But, away from the tourist trade, published reports are available on the impact of midges on other Highland industries. One report, for example, on the effect of biting midges on forestry, showed that in the west Highlands, of the sixty-five working days of summer, up to 20 per cent of the time could be lost due to acute midge attacks on the forestry gangs, with the greatest effects being seen in the plantations in areas of highest rainfall. Of all occupations in the Highlands, forestry workers suffer worst from midge onslaughts. Hand-weeding and planting both involve working close to the ground vegetation, and are notoriously prone to concentrated assaults. The work squads involved in timber harvesting have another kind of hell. There the men build up a fair sweat under their safety helmets and visors, and create an odour that attracts midges in large numbers. As long as the chain-saws are working the midges keep their distance, probably deterred by the exhaust fumes. But sooner or later the saws need re-fuelling or re-sharpening, and this is the moment when the midges move in and drive hardened foresters to near-despair. Indeed, there is an old saying among foresters that midges never attack a man standing with his hands in his pockets. But occupy his hands with a fencing maul, ditching spade or saw and the midges seem to know they can get a meal without being caught.

When the foresters return to their crofts in the evening, the midges are waiting for the intrepid soul who dares to cut or turn his hay. It is no laughing matter to see grown men raking the hay, with their heads and faces covered in their wives' nylon tights. Ex-army respirators have at times been called upon for emergency protection. Many other crofters are forced to stay inside on such evenings.

The economics of the property market in the Highlands are also affected by midges. Many a house sale has fallen through when the would-be buyer discovers just how midgy the garden becomes in summer. Indeed, one leading firm of Glasgow chartered surveyors advises clients to avoid putting their Highland houses on the market during the midge season.

Forestry and crofting are part of the predictable long-term future of the Highland economy. Both occupations are well adapted to the midge problem. What is less predictable is the return of the 15 million tourist trips made annually to Scotland, worth some £4.1 billion. Visitors to the Highlands spend over £500 million each year in the region, the greater part in the months of summer. This sum represents about 20% of the gross domestic product of the Highlands, considerably more in some tourist-favoured localities. As these valued visitors are often not aware of the midge problem until it bites them, there is a strong case for ensuring that such guests come fully prepared for the midges. That way visitors may be able to adapt quickly to the environment, enjoy their holidays to the full without feeling deceived or misled and to go home fully intending to return in future years.

MIDGE CONTROL—IN FOLK MEDICINE

Man has had something like 8,000 years in which to learn to live with midges in Scotland. From the earliest times he may have been responsible, unwittingly, for the spread of the Highland Midge. There is strong evidence that substantial areas of the Highland mainland, now covered in blanket bog, were once comparatively well-wooded and as a result comparatively well-drained. The repeated findings of preserved tree stumps at the base of the bogs together with layers of charcoal indicate that Scotland's earliest inhabitants began the process of forest destruction by clear-felling and by fire. Over several millennia, the landscape, stripped of trees and opened to erosion in the high rainfall areas, developed into the mire formations of *Sphagnum* bogs so familiar today. It is just such areas that form the core of the breeding grounds of the Highland Midge.

Alongside their first pastoral activities, the early settlers must have quickly learned how to cope with the midges. One simple but effective discovery would have been the smoky fire. The smoke from burning wood and peat appears to interfere with the highly sensitive detectors on the midges' antennae and suppresses their ability to target potential victims. Smoke remains a useful deterrent to this day. The nearest equivalent to the portable smoky fire is the pipe full of tobacco, a device widely promoted for keeping midges at bay in several nineteenth century manuals on salmon fishing. The introduction of tobacco into Scotland in the early seventeenth century may have displeased King James VI, but by then he was down in London and safely away from the midge. In succeeding years the efficacy of tobacco found a new meaning in Scotland. In the late nineteenth century English workmen were brought to the island of Rum, there to build Kinloch Castle for the Lancashire millionaire industrialist Sir George Bullough. Some 300 labourers were imported to build the castle using red sandstone brought up from the Isle of Arran. As part of their contract and despite their Accrington origins, the poor souls were required to wear Sir George's Rum tartan kilt. The midges must have been delighted by this obliging exposure of prime English leg. However, the one shilling a week kilt money was not enough to compensate for the torment of the midges and Sir George nearly had a strike on his hands, which was only averted when he agreed to pay his men a tobacco allowance of twopence a week to keep the midges at bay. Although tobacco smoking is less favoured today, the resolution of ex-smokers has been cracked by midges in the past. Queen Victoria's watercolourist Carl Haag was given the task of painting views of Lochnagar, near Balmoral. Although this respected and stalwart Austrian had publicly given up smoking months earlier, it took just one really bad midgy afternoon to compel him to send his servant back for a box of cigars.

Herbal concoctions against biting insects have a long history. The Romans used camphor, extracts of cypress, pomegranate skins, cinnamon and galbanum with a little wolfsbane tossed in, presumably as a last line of defence. The common plant mugwort

(*Artemisia vulgaris*) owes its name to the old-English mycgwort, literally midge-plant. A related species, wormwood (*Artemisia absinthium*) was recommended by Turner in his sixteenth century herbal as an insect repellent when used either as a lotion or when burnt on a fire. Both of these species are related to tropical plants which have long been exploited, commercially, for their potent insecticidal properties. The active ingredients, known collectively as pyrethroids, act in nature to deter insects from feeding on the plants. Some of these pyrethroids, particularly the modern synthetic ones, are highly toxic not just to insects but also to humans, and should be handled with care.

Over the centuries a number of plant extracts or distillations to ward off insects have been described, some of which have been shown in laboratory studies to act as potent midge repellents. By the 1920s several anti-midge nostrums had been published promoting oils expressed or distilled from a wide range of plants, including lavender, lemon, lemon-grass, fleabane, wormwood, geranium, bitter orange, white cedar, cypress, eucalyptus, dill, fennel, juniper, tansy and thyme. Despite this long list, all of these plants have in common a small number of chemically-related oils called terpenoids. Many of these terpenoids have been re-evaluated in recent years in the quest for a 'natural' solution to combating biting insects.

Several of these terpenoids, such as limonene, pinene, thujone and citronella, are, indeed, powerful repellants. All have a strong and characteristic aroma and are widely used in perfumes, shampoos and soaps. Pinene, for example, is used in household floor-cleaners to impart a smell of country freshness. Citronella and geraniol are widely employed to give a lemon-smell to shampoos. Whether or not washing with such shampoos has any effect on midges has not been recorded. Thujone, found in red and white cedars (*Thuja* spp.), does seem to have a deterrent effect on midges; the foresters in the days before chemical repellents used to

select a *Thuja* hedge or tree to have their rest under as a midge-free zone. But it was citronella which was most widely used as a pre-war midge repellent. The Forestry Commission issued gallon-jars of citronella to their workforce, right up to the 1950s. This had the reputation of turning the user an olive-yellow colour with continuous application. It has its adherents to this day and it can still be found for sale, occasionally, in Highland pharmacies.

Following the recent revival of interest in herbal alternatives to synthetic chemical repellents, some of the old remedies are once again being offered for sale. One such is marketed as a blend of natural repellents based on oils of citronella, pennyroyal, cajuput, lavender, bergamot and sassafras. Interestingly, the last component, sassafras, comes from a tree which used to be prescribed to ward off the effects of the mosquito-borne ague (or malaria). Another anti-midge repellent currently marketed contains neem oil from the Indian sub-continent where the leaves of the neem tree have long been used as a traditional insect repellent. Less exotic is bog myrtle oil, which has been more recently marketed specifically for its anti-midge properties. Unlike sassafras and neem, bog myrtle (*Myrica gale*) grows naturally throughout the western Highlands and islands and has the potential for creating a local insect repellent industry. The oil is actually a cocktail of volatile terpenoids (including pinene, limonene, eucalyptol with even a hint of citronella). Unfortunately, the commercial yield of oil from bog myrtle is low and, as with many natural oils, if applied in too dilute a form it is ineffective. The catkin-like flowers have the highest concentration of oils and there may, indeed, be some benefit, though not a commercial one, in applying well crushed leaves and flowers at least to old clothing. A recent trend among some manufacturers has been to market concentrated concoctions containing not one or two but a battery of natural compounds. At the last count one product is currently sold containing volatile extracts from no less than seven different plant species. Midges will be pleased to read that the preparation comes with assurances that it is GMO free and has not been tested on animals!

In Australia, where the coastal midges can be a serious nuisance, the Queensland sea-anglers have developed their own insect repellent. Having drunk the contents of a beer bottle or can, they half fill it with vegetable oil, add a quarter of a cupful of an antiseptic liquid such as Dettol, top up with water and shake vigorously. The foaming emulsion is then applied liberally to all exposed parts. Visiting midges may be deterred by the smell of carbolic acid or if not they will drown in the vegetable oil, or so it is claimed. The recipe has the advantage over most commercial repellents that it does not contaminate the bait nor dissolve nylon tackle. A less *macho* version uses equal parts of baby oil, Dettol and eucalyptus oil.

Each year a number of balms and costly potions are marketed as midge repellents but which seem to be more geared to attracting other humans than deterring the midge. However, one balm does seem to have useful properties. Its value was discovered in the Florida Everglades. There, both midges and other biting flies are a serious menace to visitors. Some adventurous souls found that, by swathing themselves in a bath-lotion marketed as Avon Skin-So-Soft, they were able to keep the midge bites to a tolerable level while smelling sweet themselves. It may well be that small insects simply drown in the sticky lotion, though it is true that the ingredients include at least one compound which might well ward off insects (as well as promoting soft skin). This product has for years been favoured by Highland families who stock up with half-a-dozen bottles at the start of the midge season. That bottle being passed round among the spectators at shinty matches isn't always whisky.

In the scientific literature, there are regular reports of plants which are discovered to have potent anti-mosquito (and presumably anti-midge) properties. Most of these plants come from the tropics and warmer climates though many have relatives among our native flora or among our common garden plants. *Delphinium staphisagria* from the Mediterranean region is one. *Spilanthes mauritiana* from Kenya, a relative of *Helianthus* and *Dahlia* spp. contains a powerful mosquito larvicide. It would be an interesting and useful challenge to cultivate a midge-free garden in the Highlands by trying to grow some of these species here. For those gardeners willing to try, one group of plants worth considering for their anti-midge potential are those Compositae in the tribe Anthemidae (e.g. *Tanacetum, Artemisia, Anthemis, Santolina* and others) which have long been known for their insecticidal properties. With over 1,200 species there should be plenty to choose from. A midge-free garden in the Highlands would certainly make the headlines.

But perhaps a more simple way of coping with midges lies in another characteristic common to midges and indeed mosquitoes. These insects are attracted to dark colours. Scientists have long used black cloths laid over the ground specifically to catch midges alive, for further study. One explanation for this preference for dark colours is that many midge species take their rest on dark-coloured vegetation including tree-trunks. This ties in with the crofters' claim that the old breed of sandy-coloured Highland Cattle suffered less from the midges than did the Black Cattle. This is not an observation confined to Scotland. Experienced entomologists working in Africa often trap mosquitoes and midges using black cloths. In Russia, midges have been recorded being attracted to and landing on stationary dark-coloured cars, while avoiding light-coloured vehicles. Although proper trials seem not to have been conducted, this repeatedly observed preference for dark colours should not be ignored. It makes sense then to wear light-coloured clothing whenever midges are about.

CONTROL—THROUGH CHEMICAL REPELLENTS

It was with considerable foresight that the then Secretary of State for Scotland, Tom Johnston, in 1944 asked his scientific advisors to find out if there was a suitable chemical repellent available which could be used against midges. Johnston was no doubt aware of the war-time campaigns fought against mosquitoes to control malaria and other diseases in the battle-grounds of southeast Asia. There, the allied forces were using a number of newly-released insect repellents, including one developed at the then Royal Technical College in Glasgow called di-methyl phthalate. DMP or Dimp, from army stocks held at the chemical warfare centre at Porton Down, became the subject of extensive field-trials in the Scottish Highlands. Quite what Johnston's motives were in promoting this research is not recorded. However, as an active and energetic founder and chairman of the then North of Scotland Hydro-Electric Board, he had first-hand experience of Scottish midges in the remote areas of Argyll and the Highlands. It seems likely that he would also have heard of reports that several army camps and naval shore bases in the west Highlands had become, at times, almost untenable in the midgy summers of 1943 and 1944. A mid-August walk today out to the old gun-emplacements near Aultbea will give some idea of the misery of sentry duty in those war years. One veteran, half a century later, described filling sand bags on midgy evenings as the worst of fatigues both for the squaddy holding open the mouth of the bag with two hands occupied and for man with the shovel. Both suffered the persistent attention of midges without free hands to answer back. Today, the sites abound with midges which shelter from the wind in the long abandoned war-time buildings.

Johnston's scientific advisors, drawn from each of the Scottish universities, set to work in the summer of 1945. One team undertook a large-scale survey over 18 counties throughout Scotland, to determine the number of different species present and which ones were doing most of the biting. Nine thousand specimens later the team identified one species, *C. impunctatus*, the Highland Midge, as responsible for 90 per cent or more of the trouble. Published in 1946 as a Government report entitled *The Control of Midges*, this was enough information to set the second group into action. Based in headquarters at Raigmore Hospital in Inverness, field trials of the DMP repellent were set up initially at Achnashellach, Wester Ross, and at Auchterawe, near Fort Augustus, places deep in the heart of midge country. With the co-operation of volunteers from the Forestry Commission, male and female, and with help from Land Army girls, roadmen, crofters, fishermen and school-teachers from Skye to Sutherland, a methodical testing of DMP began. Within two seasons a satisfactory formulation had been developed and tested under west coast weather conditions. Applied as a liquid or as a gel directly to the skin, or used to impregnate loose-woven veils and clothing, DMP rapidly gained approval. Its effectiveness, compared to the old pre-war repellents such as citronella, was quickly established and a Scottish manufacturer was found and from the late 1940s, DMP became available to the general public. Within a few years a second repellent appeared on the market, again from war-time anti-mosquito campaigns, called di-ethyl toluamide or DEET. Today, under EU regulations, all chemical products marketed as biocides (insecticides, disinfectants through to anti-fouling and wood preservatives) have to comply with the Biocides Directive, designed to offer protection to human users, animals and the environment. Despite the name—biocide—the product does not have to kill but can merely repel. The regulations are described more fully in the Health and Safety Executive's website *www. hse/gov/uk/biocides*. Today the compliant products on the market include compounds whose active ingredients include DEET

(N,N-diethyl-m-toluamide), Saltidin (also marketed as Bayrepel or Icaridin), IR3535 and Citrepel. Other compounds may well be registered in coming years. The products, that is the labelled brands you see on the shop shelf, have a range of names and formulations. These include old stand-bys like Jungle Formula (a DEET-containing product), and more recently Smidge (based on Saltidin). But watch what you're buying. The concentration of the active ingredient varies greatly. DEET in liquid form, for example, is present in concentrations from around 12% to 55% or even more. Surveys among British and US forces found that DEET at 75% was quite sufficient to ward off mosquitoes, while higher concentrations offered no real advantage. When marketed in the form of aerosols, however, as the propellant evaporates it leaves behind on the skin 100% repellent. In terms of value for money, liquid or spray preparations may be a better buy, particularly over gels, balms and creams. But buyer beware: the price charged for similar if not identical products can vary wildly. Several repellents also claim to offer up to ten hours protection. Try telling that to long-distance walkers with a cloud of midges in pursuit or forestry gangs, though in fairness the assertion may be valid for the more sedentary user in cool climates.

What about the active ingredients? DEET (sold as Jungle Formula and several other brands) for all its effectiveness, tried and tested over fifty years, melts plastic, spectacle frames, polished or painted surfaces, rayon or acetate. To avoid this, many users apply the liquid or spray directly onto their cotton or woollen clothing. Saltidin (sold as Smidge in Scotland) or Bayrepel (in Autan) claims to be as good as DEET but without the plastic-melting properties. Citrepel is marketed as a 'natural insect repellent', its active compound, menthane-diol, being extracted from eucalyptus, while otherwise complying with the Biocide Directive. The products sold under the name Avon Skin-So-Soft contain as an insect repellent IR3535, again Biocide Directive compliant.

How safe and effective are these repellents? Some, like DEET, have been marketed round the globe for decades, others with a less-long pedigree have been released only after rigorous testing. Apart from the relatively small number of adults with unusually sensitive skins, there is no compelling evidence to indicate that those compounds on the Biocide Directive are not safe when correctly and sensible used. Incorrectly used, however, they are harmful if, for example, they are sprayed into eyes or mouth and are toxic if ingested. It has long been recognised that many repellents, including DEET, are absorbed by the skin, passing through the liver and kidneys to reappear in the urine in a modified form hours later. It makes sense then to treat all repellents with caution. For children, repeated and extensive applications of DEET can lead to abnormal behaviour. This may be true of other repellents and most have printed warnings stating they should not be applied to children below a certain age. The British medical journal The Lancet published the following advice on the use of DEET (the journal has yet to speak on the other repellents):

> When used sensibly insect repellents are advantageous and safe, but the potential toxicity of DEET is high and the use of repellents containing more than 50% DEET should be avoided in infants and young children because of their thinner skin. Frequent total body application of DEET for days or weeks should be avoided.

These are sensible precautions which are followed by most users. One foolish Finn, however, applied 70% DEET daily to all his bare parts immediately before prancing into his open-air sauna. Within 14 days he developed acute manic psychosis. Soldiers (presumably volunteers) who applied high concentrations of DEET frequently over many days developed skin rashes, blistering and chronic contact dermatitis. Exposure to DEET has also been held, though not proven, to be partly responsible for psychological effects linked to Gulf War syndrome.

Some manufacturers have recently reduced the concentration of DEET to 50 per cent following medical comment. A perhaps healthier alternative is to apply the repellents not to the skin but to clothing (provided this is not nylon-based). The clothing will eventually become stained but at least the repellent will not be absorbed by the skin. Particularly with young children it makes more sense not to apply any insecticides directly to the skin but to apply the repellent in small amounts to clothing such as sun-hats, socks and sleeves. Because of concerns over DEET, its safety or its plastic-melting properties, or safety of any repellents that are synthetic, there are many products specifically labelled as 'natural', 'DEET-free' or 'no synthetic repellents', which are based on blends of natural plant-derived compounds, with pleasant smelling additions which have little to do with insect repulsion and more to do with customer attraction. A number of these 'natural' products seem to undergo changes in formulation and brand name each season, and this certainly raises the question why? If they are as effective as claimed on the label, why do they need to be reformulated, particularly when most are based on the same familiar half-a-dozen plant extracts? It is also important to bear in mind that most repellents, synthetic or natural, are aimed at the much larger Continental and Mediterranean holiday market, and are often targeted at mosquitoes, ticks and other pests, rather than midges *per se*. How effective they are against the Highland Midge in the field under Scottish weather is much less certain.

It has been long known that certain individuals are less prone to midge bites than most of us. Research at Aberdeen University and Rothamstead has identified compounds, truly 'natural' ones, emitted in human sweat or breath which, at least in the laboratory, interfere with host location by midges. By monitoring the electrical signals generated by the midge antennae it has been possible to distinguish those substances which are powerful repellents from those which attract, the ones which are genetically coded by those lucky individuals who suffer least from midge bites. Field trials have been held using several formulations. Prospects for a truly 'natural' repellent, both for midges and mosquitoes, are there. Another approach exploiting the extremely sensitive scent detectors on the midge antennae has been not to repel but to attract midges away from a particular location. This is not new – the bushmen of Namibia have long used tethered goats to attract tsetse flies away from camping grounds. The hapless animal, staked some distance away, attracts the flies while the humans enjoy life. The modern equivalent to the goat, developed first as a mosquito trap, is the machine which emits a chemical attractant, trapping the midges as they home in on the scent. The devices come in several makes and prices. They release warm carbon dioxide (a trigger for many blood-sucking insects) and water vapour by burning propane gas, sometimes with small additions of octenol. Midges downwind pick up the scent and home in on the machine, there to be drawn on a flow of air into a trap. Carbon dioxide and octenol are naturally present in mammalian breath and together form powerful midge attractants. Incidentally, octenol is also used in the preparation of certain perfumes and toiletries, in case you ever wondered. The devices work and certainly can catch astonishingly large numbers of midges. According to Alison Blackwell, a kilogram of trapped midges is equal to eight million females.

Ah, but then, it all depends on where, when and why the devices are being used. The capital cost of the burner is expensive and running costs are not cheap. The machines are releasing carbon dioxide, not the greenest of waste products. Operated in confined high-value locations in the lightest winds, say on a hotel patio during the evening cocktail hour or downwind of the barbeque (barbeques also attract midges) they may reduce the incidence of midge assaults. What a single device will not do is keep midges away from a large area such as a caravan park. Even in a small garden, a change in the wind direction can disperse the carbon dioxide attractant in the wrong direction, allowing upwind midges to drift into the area on to protesting guests. Even in the lightest winds it doesn't take long for midges to be carried in from a distant moorland breeding ground. However, used appropriately at the right location under suitable wind conditions, these machines may have a value.

There is, however, scope for improving the effectiveness of the currently-available repellents. In 1946, when DMP was undergoing field trials in the Highlands, volunteers were asked to wear loose-woven net cotton veils previously impregnated with the repellent. The responses were highly favourable but for various reasons, including perhaps the design or weight of the cloth, use of the veils was discontinued. The veil was in fact a revival of an old habit—Punch cartoons of the 1850s had visitors to the Highlands busily sketching nature in head veils with holes cut out for the eyes and mouth! More recently, net jackets with hoods have been manufactured and sold in the United States aimed at the hunter and game-fisher. These loosely woven, lightweight jackets come complete with press studs and draw strings. They need to be impregnated from time to time, perhaps once every few days, by simply storing the jacket in a specially designed bag containing the DEET-based repellent. They work by creating a repellent-laden aura round the wearer and not by presenting a physical net barrier to the insect. Indeed the wearer's face and hands are entirely free. Limited trials of the jacket have been conducted in Scotland, by coincidence near Achnashellach, the location of the original post-war midge repellent trials. Local people have tried out the jackets for several seasons with success, allowing gardeners to weed and crofters to turn hay late into the evenings, a task considered to be almost impossible after eight o'clock in the evening without the impregnated jacket. When freshly impregnated, the jacket is highly effective against the Highland Midge, it is comfortable to wear and does not impede movement and has the merit that there is no contact between chemical repellent and the wearer's skin. Its drawback is that it is relatively expensive and could only really be recommended for those who are likely to be exposed to severe midge attacks throughout the season. A cheaper alternative is the midge hood or veil which protects the face only. When marketed in the form of a loose weave the hood needs to be impregnated with a chemical repellent. Other types of hood are sold with a close weave: these don't need to be impregnated but rely on the tight mesh of the veil to act as a physical barrier to midges. Both types of hoods have found favour among the hill-walking fraternity and have been issued to road repair gangs. Problems over impaired vision, particularly with close mesh hoods, have been overcome to an extent though the issue of overheating on warm days has not. Wearing of the veil can often become a choice between being hot and sticky or cool but bitten! Further developments have included a complete head-to-toe suit of fine-weave nylon or cotton mesh, worn over normal clothes—the ultimate total barrier. In recent years, fly barrier screens adapted to the minute size of midges have been marketed to cover doors and windows and are used by some Highland restaurants and museums. And a word of advice, don't buy nets or hoods coloured black. Midges like dark colours.

Repellent-impregnated candles, coils, joss-sticks, electric vaporisers and repellent-laden ribbons are sometimes sold to ward off midges, but it is doubtful if their range of effectiveness is anything more than extremely localized, though campers may find them helpful, particularly when combined with a fine mesh screen over the tent door. Ultra-violet lamps are also marketed which attract and electrocute flying insects. They are, however, highly unspecific in their targeting and kill moths and many otherwise harmless as well as beneficial insects. They do not appear to make a significant impact on midge activity. Electric buzzers which claim to imitate the sound of male mosquitoes have been the subject of successful prosecutions under the Trades Description Act.

CONTROL—BY INSECTICIDES AND LARVICIDES

After the launching of the first of the post-war midge-repellents in Scotland in 1946, a science-based push was made towards tackling the major problem—how to control midges and midge breeding in areas close to human settlements. At that time almost nothing was known about the ten-month long larval stages of the midge, so the first attempts to eradicate the insect were made against the flying adult. It was already established from work carried out in the United States and in the Pacific that mosquitoes could be controlled over large areas by spraying insecticides from aircraft. However, attempts to deal with midges in a similar way had proved much less successful, at least in the Far East. In addition, the economics of employing aircraft and specialized spraying equipment for no more than two months of the year in remote areas of the Highlands compelled the scientists to look at alternative ways of tackling the adult flying midge. Barrier spraying by creating a narrow pesticide-saturated strip or corridor had been developed during the war to protect military camps from the nightly assaults of malarial mosquitoes. Strips of land 50 yards wide, frequently dripping night after night with DDT, had proved successful at keeping several mosquito species at bay. Inevitably, the decision was made to try out barrier sprays at selected sites in Scotland.

Several acres of moorland and woodland were subjected to a fog of insecticides at concentrations known to kill most insects.

The outcome was entirely unexpected. To all intents the adult midges appeared to be quite unaffected. As soon as the spraying operations were completed the midges emerged to resume their activities. It was not the DDT (or Dieldrin, Chlordane and Malathion, also used for good measure) that was at fault. In laboratory tests midges, like most other insects, were readily knocked down by these highly toxic insecticides. From investigations in the field it appeared that midges were able to avoid all contact with the insecticide spray, probably by hiding instinctively on the underside of the vegetation. This ties in with the observation that midges at rest seek out dark shaded sites. Similar results were subsequently obtained during midge control programmes overseas. From this it became clear that the diminutive midge had one up on its big cousin the mosquito. Barrier spraying was, then, spectacularly unsuccessful against the adult. However, DDT at relatively high doses did destroy most of the midge larvae in the soil—along with, incidentally, much else of the soil invertebrate population. This near-sterilization of the soil persisted for years, DDT being a notoriously persistent toxin. But, and this is the critical point, DDT and a range of now banned pesticides did not prevent adult midges coming in on the wind from nearby unsprayed sites.

If nothing could be done at the level of barrier spraying then the next target was the subterranean larval breeding sites. Apart from the fact that little was known about the larva itself, next to nothing was known about where they developed. This gap in basic knowledge was a serious drawback. It was reasoned that if the breeding areas could be located on the ground then larvicides could be targeted to just those areas supporting breeding colonies. Identifying the precise location was seen to have another benefit; the toxic sprays could be restricted to areas safely away from livestock. Under Douglas Kettle (later to become a world authority on midges) a team from the University of Glasgow set out to locate the breeding grounds. Using specially designed traps which caught the newly emerged adult it proved possible to identify with considerable precision the breeding grounds of many of the Scottish species. Some species chose muddy farmyards, others preferred shaded woodland pools, freshwater ponds or stagnant mires. The Highland Midge, however, was found in none of these. Instead it was restricted to the damper areas of rough grazing and moorland, characteristically bearing *Sphagnum* and *Polytrichum* mosses and the jointed rush, *Juncus articulatus*. These plants now became the tell-tale for the otherwise hidden larval breeding sites. Closer examination revealed the small elusive maggots buried within the top inch of soil. These were the sites where the adult midges had laid their eggs in the previous summer and which now bore next year's generation in the form of larvae.

With the continued support of the Scottish Department of Health and with help from the Carnegie Trust and, rather more quietly, the Scottish Tourist Board, battle lines were set up in the form of a Midge Control Unit under Dr Kettle, by now based at the University of Edinburgh. Throughout the 1950s, a series of field trials were conducted on the hills outside Edinburgh (convenient for the University) and at Anancaun, Kinlochewe by Loch Maree in Ross-shire, close to the notoriously midgy Glen Bianasdail. Tests with several potent larvicides showed that the degree of effectiveness at killing the larvae depended on sufficient rainfall to wash the chemicals into the soil. Without rain the insecticides were largely ineffective. However, once washed into the soil, the toxins were highly effective in reducing midge numbers. Rather more significant was the discovery that the larvicides survived in the soil for several years. These persistent insecticides, widely used 50 years ago, had toxic effects on much more than just midge larvae.

The introduction of a chemical toxin into a food chain inevitably means that animals higher up the chain, including birds and mammals, will accumulate the insecticide from their diet. Because all animals, from insects to humans, obey the same biological principles, what is toxic to an insect is frequently potentially toxic to most other forms of life where the dose is accumulated in proportion to the body-weight of the animal. The result of profligate use of these insecticides and other toxic chemicals from the late 1940s onwards was graphically recounted by Rachel Carson in her best-selling book *Silent Spring*. As governments throughout the world began to recognize the devastating effects of pesticides on wildlife by the late 1960s, attempts to control midge breeding by the use of broad-spectrum chemical sprays was largely ended, both in Scotland and overseas.

In recent years rather more sophisticated chemical insecticides have become available which are relatively short-lived and may claim to have a degree of specificity against one or a few groups of pests. These insecticides, it is also claimed, have much less harmful effects on the environment. Today, several are authorised for use in seasonal combat against mosquitoes particularly in north America. In the United States, and elsewhere, local self-help organizations have been formed to control mosquitoes, usually by methodically treating swamps and lakes using ground-based chemical fogging, or mist spraying, or by spraying larger areas from the air. No similar attempts have been undertaken in Scotland against the midge and the reason is simple enough. During the larvicide trials in Scotland in the 1950s, there was one quite unexpected finding which once again showed that the midge has one up on the mosquito. When an area had been thoroughly doused in the appropriate larvicide and the rain had washed the toxin into the soil the midge larvae were, of course, killed. However within days midge attacks were resumed. It appeared that adult midges from areas perhaps up to one mile away were moving in to colonize the sprayed zones. The only way to have eliminated these intruders would have been to extend the larvicide treatment several miles into the hills, an impossibly expensive operation. The monetary cost of such an operation confined to even the most severely affected areas would have been prohibitive. The ecological cost to Scotland's wildlife would have been unthinkable. For these reasons the use of larvicides against the Highland Midge, whether on a small community scale or over a larger land-mass, is not a practical solution to the midge problem, quite apart from the broader environmental issues.

CONTROL—THROUGH HABITAT MANIPULATION

The problem of how to tackle the midge is not confined to Scotland. Many attempts have been made overseas, occasionally with considerable success, more often with unforeseen consequences. For example, in Australia the midge breeding grounds have been tackled fairly effectively by altering the physical environment of the site. In parts of Queensland some relief has been secured by clear-felling and back-filling the mangrove swamps, or altering the steepness of the shore-line and canal-side breeding sites. By damming or draining tidal inlets, it has proved possible to destroy midge larval habitats on a long-term basis. However, even these often costly landscaping efforts have occasionally back-fired. At one Caribbean paradise development, cursed by biting midges, the local hoteliers helped to finance the drainage of a nearby mangrove swamp, known to support a thriving colony of midge larvae. Having spent much money landscaping the reclaimed area, the developers were not pleased to find a new species of midge on the wing; one which was a more vicious biter and particularly active during the evening cocktail hour. The second species had previously been unable to establish itself in the area because the conditions of the mangrove were too wet. But as soon as the site had been drained, the vicious biter found its own breeding paradise. Other developers have learnt from this experience and more successful landscaping has involved damming rather than draining the lagoons, so keeping a permanent stand of water between the midge and its chance to lay eggs. In Scotland, it is doubtful if any attempt to alter the landscape on a localized scale would be successful in the long-term. The Highland Midge appears to be more mobile than its Caribbean cousins and is capable of drifting from distant breeding grounds right into the centre of towns and villages. Built-up areas in the Highlands such as Oban, Portree, Ullapool or Stornoway can be several hundred yards from the nearest extensive breeding grounds; yet, given the right wind conditions, midges can on occasion move into the centre of these small towns and make night life most uncomfortable. Only the most extensive programme of land drainage or water impoundment is likely to have any worthwhile effect.

Man has been actively manipulating the Highland ecology for upwards of 8000 years. By 5000 years ago Neolithic human activity had removed much of the original forest cover, such as it was. The later Holocene pollen records from 3000 years ago show by then the extensive spread of moorland and damp acid grassland, linked to changing climates, and forming habitats in which the Highland Midge would have thrived. The land-use history of the Highlands underwent significant changes in more recent times particularly with the expansion of cattle grazing (and droving) in the eighteenth century to be followed by the extensive introduction of improved breeds of sheep from the 1760s onwards, leading to intensive sheep farming in the remote areas of the north and west accompanied by abrupt displacement of long-settled human communities. The introduction of the percussion shotgun and rifle after 1790 and the later popularity of deer stalking brought economically rewarding opportunities for some very extensive Highland estates to be managed primarily for sport. The establishment in 1919 of the Forestry Commission and the widespread conversion of acid grassland and moorland to forest plantation, particularly in recent years, has also created or enlarged midge-breeding habitats.

How much these changes in land use have promoted the success of midges is a matter of continued debate but it has been habitat manipulation on a commanding scale. Intuitively, it is difficult to eliminate sheep as a factor in sustaining large numbers of midges in the Highlands—these four-footed mobile CO_2-releasing, compliant and relatively abundant sources of blood meals, conveniently shorn in June, diligently maintain and extend grazed and boggy grassland throughout the egg-laying months.

Realistically, given upwards of 4 million hectares at hand, it is extremely unlikely that the midge problem in the Highlands will be lessened by habitat manipulation on anything more than the most localized level. Queen Victoria could complain of being much molested by midges above Loch Maree in 1877. Seventy years later much of the open ground of this area was given over to the forest plantations of Slattadale. There is no evidence that this area of Wester Ross has become more or less midgy with such a large scale habitat modification.

RESEARCH—FUTURE PROSPECTS

A review of the past decades of research into Scottish midges shows that much has been achieved in understanding their life cycles, ecology and behaviour, particularly those of the Highland Midge. Research into ways to eliminate midges, through chemical spraying, ceased fifty years ago. The trials had unacceptable consequences for wildlife. Instead, more recently research has concentrated more on the physiology of midges, how they interact with their environment, how they respond to hosts and host odours and how they act as vectors for diseases.

Field investigations in the past decade have revealed more of the fine detail of adult midge behaviour, what they feed on, how they reproduce and how they respond to the environment, including changing climates. Following the spread of blue tongue virus (BTV) into northern Europe and the UK, and the threat of other veterinary diseases lingering in southern Europe, research has again explored ways we might control midges. These have included introducing pathogens to larval habitats, manipulating the genetic make-up of breeding midges, chemical baiting of areas to attract midges away from high-value sites, midge-proofing farm animal housing and altering farm practices to eradicate local breeding sites. Predictably, given years of inadequate funding, asking these questions has exposed gaps in our knowledge of the link between life history and disease transmission. There is no point in pronouncing on farm or fank hygiene unless we know just what it is that encourages midges to breed in particular locations, or even how midges select sites to lay their eggs. This last is a critical point in the life cycle. What conditions promote males to form mating swarms? What part does weather play in the development of a second midsummer generation of midges? Will changing climate extend the adult midge season? Despite our ignorance, it is, however, to the credit of the few involved in veterinary research into midges that the UK responded so rapidly and successfully to the outbreak of BTV.

Left alone, the midges will continue to cause misery to visitors and locals alike. They will continue to disrupt human activity in forest plantations, in shepherding, stock-rearing and hay-making. They will displease hotel-guests, annoy game fishers and deer shooters and irritate hill-walkers, hitch-hikers and campers. On occasions, the midges will drive these good folk away with vows of never returning to the Highlands again. This is adverse publicity for the Highlands and it is, therefore, all the more strange that the agencies concerned with tourism should keep silent about the problem. Silence will not lessen the problem and lays the promoters of tourism open to charges of being less than honest. There is an alternative approach, based partly on open discussion about midges and partly on tackling the problem by using the latest scientific developments in insect control. Although biting midges will never be eradicated from Scotland short of a major climatic upheaval, there are ways of reducing the midge problem to levels which are both bearable and which will allow the full benefits of the Highlands to be enjoyed throughout the summer. We could start by being more open about midges and improving information available to tourists.

Sustained research into midge control virtually ceased in Scotland in the mid-1960s. Overseas, research has continued, particularly in the United States, East Africa and in Australia, stimulated from time to time by outbreaks of midge-borne diseases in horses and sheep and by irate local authorities and tourist boards. In addition the governments of several developed and third-world countries support research into insect control for good military reasons. Midges along with mosquitoes and black-flies can severely impede the ability of ground troops to live off the countryside, whether in northern Canada or in southern India. All this has helped to fund research into new methods of control of the local species of midge. Scotland's midge problem, though acute by any standard, does not attract its share of research and development resources. The last large-scale repellent field trials recorded in Scotland, conducted specifically against the Highland Midge, were carried out in 1947.

Midge research is hampered not by lack of scientific talent but by lack of financial support. Since the early 1960s the Scottish midge has been seen as not a serious problem or, perhaps more accurately, accepted as a problem but one with no solution. (Had Tom Johnston thought in that way then even less progress would have been made immediately after the war.) There are three areas in which co-ordinated research is required if the purely Scottish midge problem is going to be tackled. The first, and perhaps most wanting, is to establish the extent and cost of the midge problem to the social and economic fabric of the Highlands. Conducted by assessors independent of vested interest in seasonal employment or tourism and independent of the repellent industry, the survey would focus on a number of economic sectors. These would include hoteliers, tourists, static caravan operators, youth hostels (the impact on tourism), general practitioners and physicians specializing in insect-related disorders (the impact on health), forestry including the private sector, fish farming, the building trade, road workers, coast guards, electricity, transport and communication industries and crofting (the impact on Highland industries). Given this information, it might then be possible to direct efforts into particular sectors of the economy as well as identifying which industry or trade would support, financially, further research.

The second area of effort would be to assess the repellents and repellent technologies that have been developed overseas and to see if they are effective against the Highland Midge, and to compare these with some of the traditional remedies and natural repellents. Modern repellent trials conducted under strictly defined, scientifically approved, criteria need to be carried out in the field under the varied climatic conditions of the Scottish Highlands. A number of tests have evolved over the years where groups of volunteers, male and female, young and old, are asked to apply a sequence of repellents usually to one arm only and then to subject themselves to foraging midges. Ideally the volunteers should be monitored while carrying out various tasks related to their normal occupations. To eliminate the likelihood that midges might be attracted to one individual more than another, each volunteer takes turn to test each repellent. Such trials, conducted by trained technicians under medical and scientific control, have frequently shown that one particular repellent works well under one set of weather conditions or is effective against one species of midge but is less effective under other conditions or against other species. So far as is known, rigorously controlled, extensive field trials against the Highland Midge have not been conducted in Scotland since 1947. The goal of such trials would be to identify which of the modern range of repellents, natural or synthetic, are superior to DEET against the Highland Midge on its home ground, bearing in mind safety and acceptability to the user. With sound medical and scientific backing, manufacturers or importers would be given the confidence to invest in new, safer and more effective ways of tackling the midge problem. While the immediate benefit would pass quickly to the consumer, the longer-term gain would fall to those concerned with the Highland economy, including rural industry and tourism. Having provided an opportunity to assess the social and economic costs of the biting midge and having secured at least a short-term solution through modern repellents, the third and most fundamental area of research would remain.

There is much that remains unknown about the ways of the Highland Midge. We still do not know how to culture the Highland Midge in the laboratory (that unfortunately takes time and money). If radically new approaches are to be sought for tackling the midge problem, then a new understanding of the midge is badly needed, particularly in the fields of insect physiology and behaviour. Some encouraging progress has been made in Scotland in the past few years, particularly in understanding reproduction and population biology, and in determining the role of smell in midge behaviour. This is a good start but this will be wasted if this groundwork fails to find further support. British science has all too often initiated important discoveries, opening the door to others to explore the finer details from which technological exploitation develops.

While we are waiting for the benefits of research, some good things have been happening. For example, it is already possible to predict 'good' and 'bad' midgy days, at least over a few days. There is a website, *www.midgeforecast.co.uk* (or *www.smidgeforecast. co.uk*) which runs from May to September, developed from a set of algorithms linked to daily meteorological forecasts and validated by live midge-catch data from across the country. As with pollen forecasts, at least the worst of predictions are broadcast on local and national radio. Forewarned, tourists in particular should be able to plan their day so as to avoid the worst of assaults. Commonsense also plays a part. The Highlands should not be treated as though they were the Cotswolds or Yorkshire Dales. Forecasts or not, midges will be out there looking for a meal every evening and again early in the morning, throughout the season, guaranteed.

In the medium term, following the hesitant funding of recent years, exciting new developments are possible. Now that we have the technology to study the specific body odours that attract midges, can we humans interfere with this, perhaps with a counter-odour operating, preferably, over some distance? Clues are also emerging as to why midges are less attracted by the odour of some individuals more than others. Now that we know that midges emit pheromones that invite legions of other midges to join in the feeding—can we disrupt this perhaps by wearing our own personal anti-invitation pheromone attached as a badge to blouse or jacket? Now that we have some information on swarms and copulation, can we develop ways of interfering with midge reproduction, particularly at a local level? After all, beekeepers regularly use chemically-synthesized pheromones to lure their swarms. The prospects are there given the appropriate backing.

There is one area of research which perhaps has more long-term promise than any other of solving the midge problem. This is what is called 'biological control'. At its simplest this means the control (or even the elimination) of one undesirable organism by another, less undesirable, biological component. The biological component may be a predator introduced into an area because it specifically seeks out and kills the unwanted species. An example is the deliberate introduction of a cat on to a rat-infested island. We have moved on from the crude, often disastrous, biological controls of the past. Today, the biological component is often a disease, viral or bacterial, which is intentionally spread to bring about the demise of a pest species. An example is the deliberate spread of a particular virus which destroys the Pine Beauty Moth larva, a menace capable of devastating the forest plantations of Scotland. Other insect pests are being tackled, overseas, by the introduction of genetically engineered bacteria which are pathogenic to the pest in question and, seemingly, to no other. One such organism, *Bacillus thuringensis*, is a common soil bacterium which forms resting spores. These spores can be cultured commercially and sprayed on to the target pest. Inside the spores are crystals of toxic proteins which are then digested in the highly alkaline gut of the insect larvae. Because the digestive juices of each species of insect differs from other insects, the toxic crystals can be genetically modified and targeted to particular pests—at least in theory. Whether or not this pathogen would be effective against the Highland Midge has yet to be investigated. The bacterium has been used successfully under strictly controlled conditions and on a small scale against a localized population of black flies way down in Dorset.

It is also possible to transfer anti-midge genes cut from *B. thuringensis* into plants. There the genes express themselves in the plant and subsequently cause the death of insects which choose to feed upon the transformed leaves. This works well, for example in defending the tobacco plant against tobacco hornworm. To extend this powerful weapon against Scottish midges we need to discover what moorland plants are fed upon by the male and female midges. This relatively unsophisticated but essential research appears never to have reached the scientific literature (if it has ever been done).

Midges have their natural enemies, animal, fungal or bacterial, and it may be possible to use these to control the midge population. For example, midges harbour parasitic mites and probably have done since earliest times—as can be seen in mite-infested midges preserved in 70 million-year-old amber. It is the immature mite which parasitizes the midge—the adult mite feeds on some unknown prey. It may be possible to promote mite infestation at midgey sites—though we are a long way from knowing when and how midges become infested. Indeed the importation of mites as a biological control would be thoroughly irresponsible without a major research effort to establish the specificity of the mites. The midges round the Tay and the Forth on the East Coast are sometimes infected by a minute parasitic worm. The same nematodes may, indeed, form part of the midge larvae diet—a case of eat or be eaten. Some of these nematode parasites appear to specialize in living inside the midge larvae without actually killing their host. Instead the poor old midge, when it becomes an adult, develops a mix of male and female sex organs and is effectively sterile. Field trials in California where nematodes have been targeted against midge eggs have shown a significant reduction in emerging adults. However, the American nematodes appear to have a catholic taste in insect larvae and related nematodes in Europe are known not to be choosy in their diet. Limited trials have been conducted in Scotland recently but again it would be highly irresponsible to liberate nematodes on a field scale until much more is known of their biology. Increasingly, biological control methods now have to be thoroughly vetted by government agencies charged with responsibility for safety in the environment.

To overcome the objection of introducing parasites as a control method, sterilization of immature males has proved a useful technique particularly against the Mediterranean Fruit Fly, aided by the fact that the male fruit fly pupae can be separated from the female simply by body colour. Once released these males mate with females which then fail to produce a new generation. However, as laboratory techniques for culturing the Highland Midge are in their infancy—let alone the problem of sexing the pupae—it may be some years before sterilization can be developed as a practical control method.

There is, however, one over-riding problem with biological control—the Highland Midge is hugely successful because there are millions of hectares available for breeding. Money invested on introducing biological weapons to localized sites will fall foul of the same problems exposed by the use of DDT forty years ago—adult midges from neighbouring upwind breeding grounds will drift passively into treated sites and continue biting.

The inevitable question that arises when science holds out prospects of a solution is who pays for the research needed to reach development? Funding for basic biological science, today, has to compete with many other demands from medicine, veterinary science, agriculture, ecology and environmental sciences. In Britain, science funding has to be justified also on the grounds of its worth in terms of quality of life and wealth creation. One solution has been that the customer should pay. The customers, those who stand to benefit from the research, would include the local Highland communities, the summer visitors whether as transient coach parties or longer-stay hotel guests, sportsmen including game-fishermen on the Spey and climbers on the Munroes. Others to benefit would include those who earn at least part of their living from the tourist trade whether as keepers of hotels, youth hostels, craft shops or from one of the many other businesses which thrive during the summer season. The Highland industries represented by forestry, fishing, fish farming, crofting, weaving and knitting would also benefit to some degree from midge control. In addition, other groups are concerned about biting midges but may live out of the region. These will include the medical and veterinary professions charged with health care in

Scotland and the chemical and pharmaceutical industry involved in the manufacture, import and distribution of midge repellents, insecticides and related products. With such diffuse interests it is unlikely that any one sector would be willing to finance all of the research needed to alleviate the midge problem. There is then a need for a central authority to initiate and to promote research. Fifty years ago the initiative was taken by the then Secretary of State for Scotland with funding principally from the Department of Health for Scotland and the Scottish Tourist Board. Times and attitudes to community-wide problems have changed over the half-century but if the will is there to support the research, then new answers will be found to tackle the midge problem. It could benefit from a lead.

THE ECOLOGICAL SIGNIFICANCE OF MIDGES

Whatever Man has tried to do to control the activities of midges, there remains the hard fact that midges in turn have been controlling human activities for many many years. Whether or not this age-old struggle will continue in the midges' favour remains to be seen. But quite apart from their relationship with humans, biting midges have an important and enduring relationship with many of the other creatures that go to make up the natural history of the Highlands. This is part of the ecology of the midge.

At one level, midges, like all other insects, are part of a complex food web. The sheer numbers of midges, and particularly midge larvae, throughout the west Highlands, are bound to make an impact on the lives of other organisms whether as prey or as a food-source. Bats are known to feed on flying midges, but a study of Scottish pipistrelle bats has shown that, compared with dancing midges, biting midges are a trivial part of the bat diet.

THE ECOLOGICAL SIGNIFICANCE OF MIDGES

Insect-eating birds such as warblers may pick resting midges from vegetation but the impact on midge numbers is likely to be minimal. More likely, in terms of sheer biomass, midge larvae will form an important element in the food chain of soil-dwelling invertebrates, though the precise role played by midge larvae in these subterranean food chains can only be guessed at, for this is another neglected area of scientific research. It is known, however, that the midge larvae are the food source for nematode worms. Contrariwise, the omnivorous midge larvae prey heavily on other soil organisms as can be seen from their five- or six-fold increase in body length in nine or ten months. Because they are a component of one or more food chains, then any episode, natural or Man-made, which significantly alters the size of the midge larval population will inevitably have a knock-on effect on the other inhabitants of the soil. Droughts in early summer, we know, will reduce midge numbers drastically and it is highly probable that destruction of large populations of midges due to desiccation will have a profound effect on other soil-borne creatures. In a similar way, anti-midge larvicides, biological or chemical, will have an effect also upon all those soil-borne creatures which directly or indirectly rely on midges as a food source.

Leaving aside the poorly understood world of the larvae, it is the impact made by the flying adult midge which has attracted Man's attention and more often his wrath. This impact lies at the heart of the ecology of the Highlands because it directly modifies human activities. In Siberia, where biting flies are also a serious pest, ecologists have shown that midges and other bloodsucking flies are probably essential to the maintenance of the fragile tundra by ensuring that the larger grazing animals keep on the move. Forty years ago Boris Dubitskii described the key role played by blood-sucking insects in underpinning the complex ecology of the Siberian taiga and tundra—one of the least exploited biospheres on Earth. There, midges, along with other blood-sucking insects, maintain an age-old environment where large grazing animals (and humans) are kept continuously on the move, never being allowed to settle in one place, so reducing their ability to harvest, exploit and destroy the fragile ecology of the area. The enormous population of blood-sucking insects in the taiga acts as a potent form of biological control—the control this time being reversed and exerted against large mammals including humans. It is no wonder that the depths of the Siberian birch woods and conifer forests are depleted of human inhabitants. Life there is intolerable in the summer because of blood-sucking insects.

In Scotland, where conditions may not be as extreme, the Highland ecology has already suffered much from several thousand years of human exploitation but, compared with the rest of western Europe, the destruction has been relatively limited in duration and degree and, until recent centuries, has been largely confined in intensity to the lower slopes of hills and to accessible straths and glens. The principal factors at work in controlling human activity have been the climate and geology, to an extent, but particularly the powerful impact of midges as blood-sucking insects.

Midges breed in the high rainfall areas of the Highlands and depend on the high soil moisture there for survival. For the past decade or more there have been indications of changing trends or patterns in our climate, which are likely to have a significant effect on the way land is used in future, with almost inevitable consequences spilling over into the wildlife of the area. However, the impact of climatic change, particularly in the west, will depend greatly on future rainfall patterns, something climatologists have not been able to predict with any certainty. Current forecasts suggest that we face a global rise in temperature in coming decades. To maintain breeding conditions for the Highland Midge, even a mean rise of say 1.5°C over the year would require a 10 to 15 per cent increase in average rainfall to counter increased loss of moisture from the soil by evaporation. If there is no such increased rainfall, particularly in spring, then the extent of midge breeding sites might well diminish as the soil dries out. Such a prospect remains, for the moment, at best uncertain.

Today, and for the foreseeable future, midges will continue to breed over much of the Highlands in precisely the places which have long proved to be the most difficult to cultivate and maintain in a cultivated state. Here both Man and his domestic animals have struggled to secure some sort of productive and ordered life for the past 4,000 years or so. Until recently this struggle was confined largely to the most accessible coastal strips. The broader expanses of moorland, woodland and high hills have long been considered to be, at best, half-tamed. The principal reason for this is that the environment allows just a degree of exploitation before it responds by becoming even more harsh and economically less rewarding. The stripping of the natural forests from the lower hillsides in the past four millennia has left behind land which has fallen to the ever-encroaching blanket bog and ill-drained moorland. Into this impoverished landscape the Highland Midge has moved to become, today, a dominant member of the natural wildlife, far more significant than the golden eagle, pine marten or wild cat. Having achieved this dominance over the Highlands, the biting midge should be recognized as an important element in limiting human activities. Within the context of temperate western Europe, the Scottish Highlands remain one of the most under-populated landscapes with a timelessness difficult to find anywhere at the start of the twenty-first century. This is an area where humans have a foothold and no more. If, as seems very likely, the biting midge is a significant factor in limiting our grossest capacities for unsustainable exploitation then this diminutive guardian of the Highlands deserves our lasting respect.

BIBLIOGRAPHY

There are few readily available (and readable) books on biting midges, but for those who like to delve into the literature, an introductory list is provided below. It is generally possible to obtain scientific journals from the public libraries through the British Lending Library, or online for those published recently. The selection below is only the tip of the Scottish antenna, as it were. There is also a substantial literature on midges worldwide, as well as the much more extensive studies on mosquitoes.

A few of the midge literature classics, such as Edwards' *magnum opus* of 1939, Campbell & Pelham-Clinton of 1960, Doug Kettle of 1961 and the MacGregor Committee government-commissioned report of 1946 (price twopence net), which started it all, are included below for the indispensable background. (*The present author may have the last extant original of MacGregor's and his second report of 1948, and would be happy to provide a copy.*)

Borkent, A (2004) The Biting Midges, the *Ceratopogonidae* (*Diptera*) in W C Marquardt (ed) *Biology of Disease Vectors*, 2nd edn, Elsevier, Burlington

Borkent, A & Wirth, W W (1997) World species of biting midges *(Diptera: Ceratopogonidae) Bulletin of the American Museum of Natural History* **233** 1–257

Campbell, J A and Pelham-Clinton, E C (1960) A taxonomic review of the British species of *Culicoides. Proceedings of the Royal Society of Edinburgh.* **B67**, 181–302.

Carpenter, S, Mellor, P S & Torr, S J (2008) Control techniques for *Culicoides* biting midges and their application in the U.K. and north-western Paleaeartic. *Medical and Veterinary Entomology* **22** 175–187

Carpenter, S, Wilson, A & Mellor, P (2009) *Culicoides* and the emergence of bluetongue virus in northern Europe. *Trends in Microbiology* **17** 172–8

Cook, S M, Khan, Z R & Pickett, J A (2007) The use of push–pull strategies in integrated pest management. *Annual Reviews of Entomology* **52** 375–400

Edwards, F W, Oldroyd, H and Smart, J (1939) *British Blood-sucking Flies*, British Museum, London

BIBLIOGRAPHY

Hendry, G A F and Godwin, G (1988) Biting Midges in Scottish Forestry. *Scottish Forestry* **42**, 113–19

Kettle, D S (1994) *Medical and Veterinary Entomology*, 2nd edn, Croom Helm, London

Kettle, D S (1961) A study on the association between moorland vegetation and the breeding sites of *Culicoides*. *Bulletin of Entomological Research* **52**, 381–411.

Logan, J G, Cook, J I, Mordue (Luntz), A J & Kline, D L (2010) Understanding and exploiting olfaction for the surveillance and control of *Culicoides* biting midges, in Takken, W (ed) *Ecology and Control of Vector-host Interactions*, 217–246 Wageningen Academic Publishers, Wagenigen

Logan, J G, Seal, N J, Cook, J I, Stanczyk, N M, Birkett, M A, Clark, S J, Gezan, S A, Wadhams, L J, Pickett, J A & Mordue (Luntz), A J (2009) Identification of human-derived volatile chemicals that interfere with attraction of the Scottish biting midge and their potential use as repellents, *Journal of Medical Entomology* **46**, 208–219

MacGregor, A S M (1946) *Control of Midges*, An interim report of a sub-committee of the Scientific Advisory Committee. HMSO, Edinburgh

Mellor, P S, Boorman, J & Baylis, M (2000) *Culicoides* biting midges: their role as arbovirus vectors. *Annual Reviews of Entomology* **45**, 307–340

Mordue (Luntz), A J & Mordue, W (2003) Biting midge chemical ecology, *Biologist* **50**, 159–162

Roberts, A (1993) Midges in a changing Highland environment, in Smout, T C (ed) *Scotland since Prehistory*, Scottish Cultural Press, Edinburgh

And on websites:

www.culicoides.net, maintained by the Pirbright Laboratory, Institute for Animal Health

www.defra.gov.uk/foodfarm, the Westminster government's constantly changing site on farm animal disease

www.midgeforecast.co.uk offers a regularly updated forecast on midge activity in Scotland

APPENDIX

BITING MIDGE (CULICOIDES) SPECIES FROM SCOTLAND

Species	Frequency	Breeding sites	Host	Human biting	Comment
C. achrayi	Uncommon	Loch margins	Horses	(+)	
C. albicans	Common	Wetter bog areas	—		Biting habit lost?
C. brunnicans	Uncommon	Streamsides	—	(+)	Early season flier
C. cameroni	Rare	Waterfalls	—		Argyll only?
C. chiopterus*	Common	Cow dung	Cattle	(+)	Diminutive
C. circumscriptus	Locally common	Salt marshes	—		
C. clintoni	Rare	Shaded bogs	—		
C. delta	Common	Wet areas, moors	Cattle, horses	(+)	Early season flier
C. dewulfi*	Common	Dung, stables	Horses	(+)	
C. duddingstoni	Local	Loch margins	—		
C. fascipennis	Common	Wetland mud	Birds?	(+)	
C. fagineus	Uncommon	Damp soil, moors	—		
C. festivipennis	Uncommon	Damp soil	—		
C. grisescens	Common	Marshes	Cattle	(+)	Overwinters as eggs
C. heliophilus	Frequent	Sphagnum bogs	Sheep, dogs	++	Daytime flier
C. impunctatus	Abundant	Wet acidic grassland	Cattle, deer, horse	+++	The Highland Midge
C. kibunensis	Frequent	Marshes, loch margins	Horses, birds		[synonym C. cubitalis]
C. lupicaris	Uncommon	Exposed mud	Cattle, horses	(+)	Common late August
C. manchuriensis	Uncommon	Salt marshes	—		Biting habit lost?
C. maritimus	Locally common	Salt marshes	—		
C. newsteadii	Locally common	Coastal brackish pools	—	++	Painful biter in Gairloch [synonym C. halophilus]

APPENDIX: BITING MIDGE SPECIES

Species	Common	Farms, fanks	Horse, cattle, sheep	Biting habit	Vector of *Onchocera cervicalis* in horses
C. nubeculosus	Common	Farms, fanks	Horse, cattle, sheep	+++	Vector of *Onchocera cervicalis* in horses
C. obsoletus*	Abundant	Garden compost	Cattle, sheep	+++	Mainly Lowlands
C. pallidicornis	Frequent	Marshes, ditches	Horses, birds	(+)	Especially Lowlands
C. pictipennis	Common	Woodland pools	Birds	(+)	Early season flier
C. poperinghensis	Rare	Tay salt marshes	—		
C. pulicaris*	Locally common	Muddy marshes	Horses, cattle, sheep	+++	Sweet itch of horse
C. punctatus*	Frequent	Muddy marshes	Horses, cattle, sheep	+	Sweet itch of horse
C. reconditus	Uncommon	Not known	—		[synonym *C. riouxi*]
C. riethi	Locally common	Forth, Tay salt marshes	Horses		Daytime flier
C. salinarius	Uncommon	Salt flats	—		Common on Beauly Firth
C. scoticus	Rare	On fungi?, wetlands	—		
C. segnis	Uncommon	Not known	—		
C. stigma	Common	Exposed mud	Horses	+	
C. vexans	Locally common	Damp soil	—	++	Suburbs, enters houses

Key: Biting habit: +++ = persistent biter of Man, ++ = opportunistic biter of man, + = less frequent biter of Man, (+) occasionally bites Man. — = most common biting habits in Scotland not known. * = species implicated as possible vectors for blue tongue virus (BTV) serotype-8 in north-west Europe.